EDUCATED AMERICAN WOMEN:

SELF-PORTRAITS

Educated American Women: Self-Portraits

by ELI GINZBERG

and ALICE M. YOHALEM

COLUMBIA UNIVERSITY PRESS

NEW YORK & LONDON 1966

Str 595/300/1/11/67

IN MEMORY OF

Pennerton West and John L. Herma

FOR YOUR GOODNESS *IS* AS A MORNING CLOUD

AND AS THE EARLY DEW IT PASSETH AWAY

Preface

This is the third and final volume which presents the results of studies of talented persons initiated in 1960 by the Conservation of Human Resources Project at Columbia University.

At first the research staff used the term "talented" to describe the men and women who had won graduate fellowships at Columbia University during the 6 years following the conclusion of World War II, that is, between 1944–45 and 1950–51. The primary objective of this research, which was supported by the Carnegie Corporation, was to learn what had happened in the intervening decade and a half to these intellectually capable individuals in the pursuit of their careers. Our method for eliciting information was the use of a carefully constructed questionnaire.

We were not very far along in our analysis of the early replies when we noted that a high proportion of the women respondents were taking us to task for the inadequacy and inapplicability of our questionnaire for them. They contended that, because of its many questions about continuous work experience, it was relevant primarily to the study of men. Upon reflection we found that we agreed. We therefore excluded women from that study and concentrated on bringing the investigation of talented men to a successful conclusion. The results were published under the title *Talent and Performance*, Columbia, 1964.

In 1963 we obtained a grant from the Rockefeller Brothers

Fund, supplemented by another in 1964, to carry out a parallel investigation of talented women. Having been forewarned by our first female respondents, we devised a new questionnaire which broadened our focus from an exclusive consideration of career development to a concern with life styles.

The questionnaire that we developed ran to nine pages and contained forty questions concerning the major aspects of the respondents' lives. At the end of the questionnaire we appended several blank pages which the respondents were encouraged to use to provide additional information about their life circumstances and attitudes.

We asked our original group of women fellowship winners to supplement their initial replies, and we added to the number of the sample by including scholarship winners and other graduate students with high academic standing. Three hundred and eleven women responded to this questionnaire.

The analysis of this group has been published under the title *Life Styles of Educated Women*. That volume presents a detailed examination and evaluation of the family background, education, marital status, work history, occupational achievement, values, expectations and satisfactions of these 311 highly educated women. Women whose autobiographies appear in this volume were among these graduate students who attended Columbia University 15 to 20 years ago and who had been adjudged by their professors to be outstanding pupils.

One of the striking differences between our men and women respondents was the much greater disposition of the women to elaborate their answers, often to the point of supplementing them with pages of typescript. They were more introspective in their replies and more articulate than the men who had, of course, received a questionnaire covering a less inclusive range of concerns. Many of the women clearly welcomed the invitation to write fully about themselves.

It was this latter characteristic that stimulated us to plan a

volume of self-portraits. The material that was available
seemed to ask to be used. However, there always are several
important steps between the idea of a book and the finished
product. In this instance, a selection had to be made from
among the 311 life histories. We thought it desirable to select
portraits that would reflect the wide range of life experiences
that was exhibited by this group of women. We were not concerned about how representative the selections were, especially
since in the companion volume, *Life Styles of Educated
Women*, the canons of scientific inquiry were followed.
Therefore, we deliberately selected life histories which were
informative and revealing. It should be noted that had we not
imposed a limitation on the number of portraits, there would
have been at least an equal number of additional reports of similar interest and quality.

We have woven together the brief replies to the two-score
questions and multiple sub-questions in the questionnaires and
the extended final remarks so that they resemble self-portraits.
We had been confronted with a similar challenge some years
earlier in our large-scale investigation called *The Ineffective
Soldier: Lessons for Management and the Nation* (1959).
The second volume of that study, entitled *Breakdown and
Recovery*, was constructed from similar materials. However,
these were not primarily autobiographical. Here, we have constructed the life stories in the words and styles of the respondents, adding only that minimum of connective material
necessary to weave the discrete replies into an intelligible
whole.

When we originally elicited the cooperation of these
women we assured them that we would treat their replies to
the questionnaire in a confidential manner and that their experiences and reflections would appear only as an anonymous
part of a larger whole. How could we reconcile this assurance
with the publication of a series of self-portraits? We left this

up to the women themselves. Each subject of a portrait was informed of our project and provided with a copy of her life history as we hoped to publish it. These contain disguises that alter all identifying data except in a few cases where the subjects preferred that no such changes be made. We received permission to use all the self-portraits included in this volume.

In developing the disguises, our objective was to make it impossible for the reader to identify the respondents. But we were careful not to change the substance of any case. Before it was adopted, each contemplated alternative was carefully weighed to insure that it did not distort the individual's life and experience. We can say that each woman has been thoroughly disguised but that her experiences have not been altered in any fundamental way.

While these self-portraits are composed exclusively of first-hand information obtained from the questionnaires, no respondent would have written her autobiography in quite this way. There are many facets of each woman's life that were not elicited in the questionnaire, or were dealt with only cursorily. But what the portraits lack in fullness and depth may be compensated for by the sharpness of their focus and the lack of contrivance, which have often proved to be major hurdles for the writer of autobiography.

Dr. John L. Herma and Carol A. Brown, who have been involved in our several studies of talented persons, contributed substantially to the shaping of the present volume. Professor Ivar E. Berg and Sherry Gorelick, through their discerning comments at each stage of the research, also contributed.

Ruth Szold Ginzberg edited the manuscript for press and in the process contributed to its readability.

ELI GINZBERG

September, 1966

Contents

EDUCATED AMERICAN WOMEN:

SELF-PORTRAITS

A World in Change

The lives that women and, for that matter, men, lead reflect two sets of major forces. The first is composed of the external environment with its complex of opportunities and constraints. The second reflects the values and goals of the individual who, always with some margins for discretion, must determine what he most wants and the price he is willing to pay for it.

The extent of transformation which takes place in the role of women is an important index of the rate of social change. The more rigid the society, the more fixed is the pattern of life which women must follow. In the United States, major changes have occurred in the structure and functioning of society during the present century, and these have led to fundamental transformations in the patterning of women's lives.

Changes in the lives of educated women in the post-World War II decades can be appreciated only against a background of the more important changes that took place during the preceding generations in the world of work on the one hand and in the home on the other.

By the turn of this century the United States was well on the way to becoming an industrialized urban society. The majority of the population lived in urban centers. The factory system was well established. The tertiary stage of economic development—the expansion of the service sector—was proceeding rapidly while the number engaged in agriculture was nearing its peak and manufacturing was still experiencing a rapid growth.

As our society became more urbanized and as the service sector of the economy grew, the restricted life pattern followed by most women began to give way. Six factors can be singled out that have cumulatively changed the basic structure of woman's relationship to the world of work.

The first and possibly the most important factor has been the development of a great number of jobs which are particularly well suited to women. These have sprouted in many different sectors of the economy. In manufacturing, there has been a marked shift from heavy to light work, which means that women are able to meet physical demands, sometimes even better than men. Expansion of retail trade and of the communications industry also has increased opportunities for women workers. In addition the beginning of this century saw the rapid growth of the educational and health industries, for which women are well suited.

A second factor has been the expansion of secondary school and college education. Unlike European girls, girls in the United States have long shared with boys access to education. As free educational opportunities have been expanded, girls as well as boys have had access to them, surely through high school. As a matter of fact, for many decades, more girls than boys have graduated from high school. While the proportion of female graduates is reversed in college, young women have long comprised a significant minority of the college population. The increased educational achievement of women has given a double stimulus to the employment of women. Many young women are undoubtedly stimulated to find an outlet in work for the knowledge and skills which they have acquired, and in turn their education and training make them a potentially attractive manpower resource.

The ways in which people behave are changed by new ideas

which come to dominate a society. Prior to World War I it was generally believed and accepted that the place of a married woman was at home. But wars have a way of uprooting hallowed traditions; with the manpower scarcities of World War I, some of the prejudice against married women working out of the home dissolved. The post-war era witnessed the removal of additional constraints that had previously shackled women. But the real breakthrough came when the manpower needs of World War II propelled many married women out of their homes and into factories and offices.

A further factor in removing these constraints has been the diffusion of the knowledge of birth control techniques throughout much of the population, with a corresponding decline in the average size of families. This has also made it possible for women to determine when to have children. No longer must a woman devote three or more decades to child rearing. She can collapse the span of years previously devoted to maternal responsibilities. And many have done just that.

Closely related to the foregoing has been the lightening of the burdens of homemaking as a result of the steady and substantial rise in the standard of living and steady advances in the technology of housekeeping, previously so time-consuming and physically exhausting. While women, if they wish, can continue to fill their days by taking care of their homes, electrical appliances and packaged foods permit them to economize markedly on the time and energy which they previously devoted to domestic duties. And many have taken advantage of the opportunities thus presented to reallocate their time and get jobs outside the home.

The sixth change that has contributed to accelerating the entry or reentry of married women into the world of work has been the shift in the attitudes of men. In the past many husbands objected to their wives' working because, among other reasons, they thought it reflected on their ability to support their families. This is no longer true. Some men still discourage it but, since so many married women now work —about 13 million have some kind of job during the course of a year—and since society at large tolerates, even approves of, the new trend, we may assume that few men actually oppose their wives' working. Among educated men, the number who now encourage their wives to take jobs is probably greater than the number opposed to their working, since they are more likely to recognize the need for fulfillment outside the home.

These then are the principal forces that have been operating since the beginning of this century to change the larger environment which shapes the lives and work of all women. Such radical transformations in the environment have had a most important effect on the way in which women today set their sights and order their lives.

However, these broad changes in the environment at large merely set the limits within which plans and adaptations are carried out. A second set of forces, individual values and goals, is of equal importance in influencing a woman's style of life. The specific life patterns that a woman develops depend on three strategic variables: the shaping of her personality, the immediate circumstances of her adult life, and the way in which she responds to these circumstances.

Although a woman's genetic endowment is, of course, crucial to the character of her personality, the environment in which she grows up determines in considerable measure the type of goals and values she develops. The most significant influence is the family into which she is born and reared. Her parents play a large role in the determination of the amount and type of education she acquires and this, in turn, affects her interests and outlook. Her parents' values influence her definition of her future role. They can encourage the development

of a goal which stresses a career or marriage, or a balance between a career and marriage. They can provide a home that
stimulates the development of ideas, interests, and capacities or
one that furnishes limited opportunities for self-realization.

Other persons, adults and peers, also play important roles in
personality development. So, too, do such institutions as
schools, churches, and recreational groups, whose programs
may affect the shape of a young girl's aspirations. Eventually,
from all the influences to which she has been exposed, each
woman develops a set of values and goals which contributes to
the pattern and direction of her life.

No matter what plan a young woman develops for her life
and work, her ability to realize her goals will be influenced by
the circumstances of her adult life. If she remains single, she
usually has no choice but to support herself by engaging in full-
time work. If she marries while she is in school, her husband's
income may help to determine the extent of her education,
since she may have to interrupt her own studies to help him to
complete his. After she has her children, her husband's earnings will largely determine whether she can afford household
help which in turn will affect her ability to hold a job.

Her husband's career may impose limitations on her own
work. If he is transferred frequently, it may be difficult even
for a well-prepared woman to pursue her career systematically
because of limited opportunities in many communities. A
woman often marries a man in the same or an allied field and
she may find that many institutions, especially colleges and
universities, will not hire more than one member of a family.

The husband himself can also exercise a determining influence
on the patterning of his wife's work and life. If he holds a negative attitude about a woman's working, he may interpose so
many objections that his wife will forego a career in order to
save the marriage. Another husband may take a diametrically

opposite stance; he may push his wife into further education and work even though she prefers to remain at home with her children.

Another significant set of circumstances results from the presence of children. Depending on the number and, particularly, the ages of her children, a woman is under more or less pressure to adjust the pattern of her life to their needs and demands. While, as we have noted, a woman can regulate the number and spacing of her children, she cannot always predict the constraints and pressures that a growing family may exert on her plans for a career.

We see, then, that her husband's income, his job, his attitudes, and the needs of her children all go far to determine the character of a woman's activities. In addition, there are restrictions due to the fact that many employers are reluctant to hire women.

The third determining factor is the response that a woman makes to the particular circumstances she encounters. There are many different ways in which women can cope with the same objective circumstances. For instance, one woman may decide to work only if taking a job will yield the family a net increment in income. Another may decide to work as long as taking a job costs her nothing. In a family with some margins, a woman may work even if her salary does not cover the expenses incurred by her employment.

Some women are willing to leave their children to the care of a maid; others will work only if a close relative cares for the children; still others insist upon bringing up their children themselves.

Some women who want to combine home and work will put forth a great amount of physical and emotional effort in order to meet their responsibilities in each sphere. Others will not or cannot expend so much energy and time; they either cut down their obligations at work or cut corners in their homemaking or make adjustments in both. Some mothers wish to spend their free time in paid employment; others choose to utilize their skills and pursue their interests by engaging in volunteer work or in creative leisure activities; still others think of homemaking and child rearing as full-time activities.

These are some of the many different ways in which women respond to given sets of circumstances. Their responses are determined by a type of balance sheet of sacrifices and rewards. This reflects, first, the importance each woman attaches to realizing specific values and accomplishing specific goals in the various areas of her life. In addition, the entries reflect the costs which she ascribes to different actions which she must take to realize her values and goals.

Before the turn of the century alternative patterns of life were determined to a great extent by a more or less rigid environment. A woman who had completed higher education could generally pursue a career only at the cost of foregoing marriage and a family. If she married she had to withdraw from work and devote her abilities and energies to raising her children and participating in voluntary activities. Her alternatives were a career *or* marriage.

Because of the revolutionary changes which have taken place in the environment, these limited alternatives have been significantly broadened. A woman is now able to work while she is studying, before her marriage, after she marries, while her children are very young, after they enter school, or after they have grown up. Or she may decide not to work. Moreover, even if she decides to follow one pattern, she can shift to another. For example, if she finds that her decision to work while her children are very young is unsatisfactory she may resign from her job. Or the reverse may happen. She may stop working at the birth of her first child anticipating that she will remain out of the labor market until her youngest child enters grade school, only to find that she cannot tolerate a life of total domesticity.

The highly educated women in our study were graduate students at Columbia University at some time during the six years following World War II. They include fellows, scholarship winners, and other students with high academic standing, as described in the Preface. This study is a part of the results of a broader study of talented persons undertaken by the Conservation of Human Resources Project at Columbia University in the early 1960s. From our study of the women in this group, we were able to identify four major patterns of life. The patterns were revealed through our examination of the women's anticipations as they were clarified with time, of the actions they took as their lives progressed, and of the relationship between their goals and the realities they confronted. Each pattern is distinctive, but within each there is a great variety of goals and values, of life circumstances and of responses. The twenty-six portraits in this volume have been organized according to these four life styles.

The first group is called the *planners*. These are women who usually know what they want fairly early and who arrange their lives in order to realize their goals. They take advantage of opportunities which bring them closer to their objectives and they avoid becoming enmeshed in situations and circumstances that could deflect them. Many of their actions are conscious and deliberate, but much is outside their direct knowledge and control. Nevertheless, a retrospective view of the way in which the lives of this group unfold reveals an underlying consistency in their decision-making.

Next come the *recasters*. These women, like the planners, know what they want and set out to accomplish their objectives. But, at some point, they encounter opportunities which permit them to consider more attractive goals or they come face to face with obstacles that force reconsideration of their original aims. At this point, they reopen the entire question of their life plans and make changes in them.

The third type of pattern is that of the *adapters*, so named because they recognize early the inherent fluidity of a woman's life and avoid committing themselves irrevocably to any particular goal. They have preferences but their planning is deliberately open. They want to be in a position to respond flexibly to the circumstances and conditions which they encounter. They are less strongly committed to any particular pattern of work or life than either the planners or the recasters except for a commitment to adapt, which is a stance in its own right.

The fourth and last type is the *unsettled*. This is a composite group of women who start as planners or adapters but who have not satisfactorily resolved their search for a meaningful career or marriage or both. They are still groping. Some made early decisions about work or marriage but found them unworkable. Now they must search for new and more satisfactory solutions.

Twenty-six life histories cannot possibly cover all the variations within these four major groups. The examples which we will present are illustrative rather than exhaustive. They portray the ways in which some women in each category have shaped their lives. As we noted earlier, they were selected because they are informative and interesting, not necessarily because they are representative.

We shall present descriptions of the general characteristics of each type and we shall summarize some of the more important features of the self-portraits that illustrate the type. We hope that in this manner we will isolate significant elements in the succession of life stories without distracting from the intrinsic interest of the autobiographical material.

The Planners

We have used the term planners to describe women who follow a pattern that is directed toward the realization of particular goals and who remain steadfast in their dedication to these aims. It is their purposefulness and direction that suggest this term. These are women who know where they are going.

Women in this group do not necessarily anticipate in detail at an early age the kind of lives they hope to pursue, and they do not consciously and rationally weigh each decision in light of their goals. A few proceed in a deliberate manner, but most do not. Nevertheless, we can classify all of them as planners because the actions they take and their reactions to their experiences reveal an unfolding quality in their lives. They have established more or less definite goals and they direct their efforts toward their chosen destinations. What they do and what they fail to do is directly related to the ends they seek.

Planning is not a one-time act. It is a process that may continue throughout a lifetime. A woman may have her sights set on a specific long-range goal, such as success in the career of her choice. At the opposite extreme, her goals may be less precise, such as an intention to leave her job at the birth of her child. Such a limited goal may make no provision for plans for later periods of her life; new plans will have to be formulated in the future.

One of the most important features of the planfulness of these women is their care to take only those actions that are consonant with their general goals and values and to avoid any involvement or commitment that might limit their freedom of action. A planner who is intent upon acquiring a maximum of education and in pursuing a career may turn aside attractive proposals of marriage which might deflect her from her goal. On the other hand, a woman who is bent upon acquiring a husband and children may abandon career opportunities in order to take up homemaking responsibilities. The age when a woman is ready to consider marriage, and the size of her family, may be integral parts of a broader design. The source of this planfulness is a clearly structured system of values which allows these women to order their goals and their lives in accordance with what is more important and what is less important to them.

It is not the content of her decisions that determines whether a woman is a planner. One woman may seek early marriage and children as basic to her happiness, while another avoids personal ties as possible interferences with her career plans. One may wish to work after marriage while another prefers to devote her time to her home and family. But it is the clarity of her goals and her deliberateness in seeking to realize them that determines whether a woman is a planner.

As the following life histories indicate, our planners can be differentiated as follows: those whose lives are organized around their preparation for and pursuit of a career; those whose goals are family oriented and who hope to realize themselves primarily through their husbands and children; and those who wish to combine work and family. Irrespective of the nature of their goals, all of those whose life histories are recorded on the following pages have one thing in common: Their planfulness provides the dynamic element in the unfolding of their lives.

THE CAREER-ORIENTED

With the increasing growth of opportunities for education and careers for women that has characterized the twentieth-century United States, it is not surprising that many women prefer to seek their primary fulfillment in the world of work. As we have noted earlier, during the last several decades there has been a social revolution in attitudes toward women who work. In addition, since World War II society has begun to manifest increased tolerance and approval of the working mother. The obverse of this changing climate of opinion is the noticeable relaxation that has come to characterize the planning of women with respect to marriage and motherhood.

A woman is no longer dependent upon marriage for her status. Some women deliberately choose to remain single, and others can contemplate without undue tension and stress the fact that concentration on educational and career goals may mean that they will never marry. Many have come to realize that they can have an emotionally satisfying life without the bonds of matrimony. Others who do marry prefer to remain childless rather than risk interference with their career aspirations, and still others are willing to postpone marriage despite the fact that delay may result in childlessness. Finally, there are those women who do marry and have children, but whose major efforts are directed toward their career activities.

Social revolutions always have antecedents and sometimes the prelude is a long one. Families who had positive views toward their daughter's preparing for a career were in the vanguard of the much larger group who today encourage their daughters in this direction.

Parental opposition, on the other hand, does not necessarily result in the frustration of a girl's career goals. Often she is able to overcome family criticism, but sometimes she must estrange herself from her family if she is not to submit to the restrictions they impose. She is able to do this because the pursuit of an education or career is no longer considered deviant; there is, consequently, social support, if not family backing, for her endeavors.

A significant fact about all of these career-oriented women is that their pattern is the one that most closely resembles that of men. As with most men, their careers are central to their planning. And, as with most men, other sectors of their lives, although important, tend to assume subsidiary positions.

Nancy Graves

My family background is not altogether unique. There are many American families in which the women have always been expected to cultivate their talents and play a necessary role outside the usual one of housewife. My grandmothers and great-grandmothers ran plantations while the men were off fighting wars or sitting in legislature; they were in charge of the grist mill or the general store, while the men ran the farm or ranch; they were the local animal doctors before there were veterinarians; one was a botanist and specialist of some repute in medicinal herbs; as teachers or ministers' wives in Western missions, they played important roles; one was left a widow, ran a large cattle and sheep ranch, and reared ten of her own children, four of her sister's children and three tramping boys who came in the depression of '93. I don't believe it has ever occurred to anyone on either side of the family that a woman could be or ought to be "a mere housewife," and hardly a man in the family would be likely to choose a wife who saw herself in that single role. It is a family in which every woman is supposed to be *somebody*.

I was born in 1915 and raised in a small Midwestern town where my father was a high-school principal. Both my parents were college graduates and my father had attended graduate school as well. My mother was a musician and, primarily out of personal interest, worked part-time as a church organist until I was about 12, when an arthritic condition prevented her from continuing. She always encouraged my interest in working, and it was taken for granted that I would have a career; I believe she has received much vicarious satisfaction from my career. I can never recall my parents expressing any expectations for me other than that I should get as much education as I wanted, find interesting work, and have a happy marriage. I have satisfied all but the last of these, which is a fair batting average. They never seemed overly concerned about marriage or the prospects of marriage for me, come to think of it.

I entered the State University in 1933, where I pursued a general education program in an integrated liberal arts setup, one of the earliest of its kind. While I found the program most rewarding and helpful in my career development, it was difficult to focus my career plans readily, both because there was little compulsion to do so in the program itself, and because my background always fell short of some of the expectations of employers interested in people with a highly specialized professional education. However, I have never encountered any lack of opportunities for work which requires integration rather than specialization, and have usually been able to adapt myself to the specialized skills demanded or to adapt the job to my peculiar interests. On the whole, my interest and participation in general education has been a tremendous asset, even though I could not successfully compete for some things I wanted in my career.

My family had a difficult time during the depression. I helped somewhat through part-time work as a student assistant during my freshman year. This led to my present interests, since the professors under whom I worked encouraged study and experience in educational research. After I graduated, I entered Columbia in order to work for my M.A. I had decided to enter social group work and graduate education was required. Anyway, I had always expected to get a graduate degree. I was interested in religious activities in college, and in New York I worked part-time at a local YWCA as a group work assistant. After I received my master's degree, I went to work as a Girl Reserve secretary in a New England YWCA. This was a good entry into my desired occupation, and I liked the salary ($1,600) and the location. I left during the war because of my mother's illness, but I served in a similiar capacity in a YWCA near the family home. I found this position to be a dead end geographically and professionally; there was poor supervision, a lack of adequate program resources, and lack of freedom for development.

I decided to enter college and university work and became a university YWCA director and assistant counselor for women. Here I had excellent supervision and an opportunity to do teaching, experimentation, and research. From this position I went to the national staff of the YWCA. This meant a substantial advancement and salary increase and I particularly enjoyed the opportunity to write. But my university experience made me want to undertake further training so that I would qualify for a college position.

I applied for fellowship aid to continue my graduate education and received a grant for further study at Columbia. I found an interdisciplinary program in philosophy and education which suited my interest in relations among academic disciplines. Thus, I was able to study subjects offered by both Teachers College and the Columbia Graduate Faculties. My professional interests in teaching, research and writing were never very clearly focused in this course of graduate study. But as these have matured and become more clearly defined, I find that my education, both undergraduate and graduate, has provided more than adequately the specialized skills necessary. Over and above these, however, it has provided a feeling for interrelationships of different institutional functions, and for relations among intellectual methods and academic disciplines that have added tremendous strength and interest to my work and provided direction for the development of my career.

I had thought of teaching philosophy or philosophy of education, but was urged to enter college administration, because of the shortage of personnel and my previous experience and interest. I found a university position in student personnel, in which I could also teach and, more important, participate in experimental administration. Two years later I became Dean of students at a small liberal arts college where I also taught counseling and engaged in a study of referral techniques. Because of a change of administration and the severe illness of my mother, coincident with health problems of my own, I was forced to resign 3 years later. However, soon afterwards, I was able to take a position as assistant to the president of a university where I was able to organize a new service and advise on special administrative problems.

I left when there was a change of administration and since then I have been in student personnel at a new branch of a state university. This position meant an advance in salary, an opportunity to build a new program on new principles in a new university from the very beginning, and association with outstanding professional people and close friends. I am in charge of residence, vocational guidance, and financial aid. My deepest satisfactions from work are in contributing to the development of students, developing research and teaching programs, and earning money. It is gratifying to watch a new institution develop, being free to experiment without having to consider what was done last year. However, we are still short of budget and manpower, which occasionally requires giving up major blocks of the program.

A problem for me accentuated by my breadth of interest has been a tendency to overinvest in work and take on too much on the job. This has occasioned health problems, and so I have had to learn to control this tendency. However, control has been easier because of the wealth of alternative activities available and because I have benefited from my academic work in physiology and psychology. This improved control has made my work more effective and enjoyable.

Professionally, my status and income exceed my expectations and, personally, my activities and interests have appreciably broadened to include such things as painting and politics, which did not particularly interest me earlier. Within my work, I find that my expectations have been exceeded in that I have been able to use my experience in general education and instruction to work toward a closer relation between personnel administration and teaching, and to apply psychological theory and philosophy to student personnel programs. In this connection, I encountered administrative resistance to the introduction of more extensive referral for counseling and psychotherapy and was able to develop a program only after I had undertaken an extensive independent study of psychoanalytic-psychiatric techniques and theory and after consultation on special problems of resistance to therapy and referral.

I have not been particularly concerned either with assistance from others in the profession or with obstacles as a consequence of my being a woman. Perhaps my attitude and expectations were naive, but I felt that I had to earn assistance and overcome obstacles by my own performance.

I am presently well satisfied with my position. However, I might leave if there were a change in administrative policies or practices, if I were unable to carry out my responsibilities adequately, or if I were offered a higher-paying or top-level administrative position. I thought of doing straight research in education but rejected the idea when I was given the opportunity to combine research and teaching with administration and found my salary and associations with colleagues I admired most satisfactory. My articles and publications have helped me get several jobs I wanted, and research has sharpened my interest in my profession and opened up new professional contacts and activities.

I believe I am working at a level that is commensurate with my abilities. Factors contributing to my achievement have been the breadth of my educational background, the support of interested and influential friends, and a high degree of flexibility and geographic mobility. I believe that my major handicaps have included lack of customary specialization, lack of aggressiveness and consistent drive, and my emotional and financial involvement with my parents. Until the last few years, I felt that I had to spend a great deal of time with them, and this feeling forced me to accept higher-salaried jobs over other more desirable ones when the former were offered and curtailed the income available to me for conference attendance, travel, and other means of professional advancement. This led me to write in order to have an additional source of income. Also, on two occasions, I felt I had to give up a desirable job in a community which I enjoyed in order to be near my mother, whose health was precarious. I also gave up an opportunity to administer a university abroad because of my mother's illness and possible family need for my presence in case of emergency. However, I have no regrets about this, since without going abroad I had at the time just as much fun and probably better experiences, and I would not have my present job if I had gone.

I have my own home and enjoy cooking, gardening, and entertaining when I am able, but I deplore the lack of time to relax and enjoy my home. During my college years, I was sure I wanted to marry and I wanted to choose someone who could share my interests and whose interests I could share. I felt that I could not give up a career in order to marry. I was equally certain that I did not wish to engage in career rivalry, nor to dominate the career of a husband, any more than I wished to be dominated. I have not married, but I feel my personal relationships with men in the profession have been facilitated by some of these expectations and anticipated problems.

I would have been a very unhappy woman without a higher education and a career because I have scholarly ability and have wanted to develop it as far as I could. I cannot say whether I would be happier if I were also married—the hypothesis is untestable, since one cannot be at once married and unmarried! I enjoy being a woman; I enjoy working with both men and women; I believe I enjoy my professional relationships with men partly because I am a woman and "vive la différence!"

The discussion of the problem of women's roles seems rather fruitless to me. We are past the age when our culture can afford sex differentiation in roles, if, indeed, this country ever fully supported it. Men play multiple roles; so do women. The problem now revolves around the source of rewards and support in the culture for multiple functions for both men and women. Not "whether" but "how" they play these roles seems to be the appropriate question. I find that much of my satisfaction, at work and in personal life, derives from multiple roles.

I feel, too, that an important social gain might be made by giving some attention to ways in which relationships between men and women can be used to improve efficiency and enjoyment in work. There may be sex-related "styles" of work which could be used to reinforce the effectiveness of both men and women on the job. The affectional aspects of on-the-job relationships, for example, may be an important factor in motivation and reward for both men and women. The office jokes about secretaries and bosses, like many jokes, might have some serious implication for real values that might be explicitly defined. The fact that the folklore indicates that these relationships may interfere with efficiency might also suggest the usefulness of exploring resources contributing to efficiency. The very useful studies of reciprocal roles in marriage and their effect on children's role expectations might be matched by studies of reciprocal men-women roles and personal styles of operation on the job. The institutional patterns within which employees operate might thus be based on more nearly accurate knowledge of the varying life styles and work styles of both men and women. Women may stand to gain more from more varied and flexible work patterns, but men might also gain from such findings.

A great deal of my professional work has been concerned with the adaptation of women to institutional patterns and vice versa. One of my functions has often been to interpret to men some of the peculiarities of women (especially particular women), and my male colleagues have often interpreted to me some of the peculiarities of men (especially particular men). If we knew more about sex-related or individually determined variations in role behavior, both my colleagues and I could do a better job. And possibly we could teach both men and women some of these factors, to the end that our society would secure more professional workers, through giving them more satisfactions on the job and a better fit between career and marriage.

It is interesting and gratifying to review a rather checkered career and see that it does make sense and show a pattern and direction. My education was made to order, both for the profession of college administration and for my personal enjoyment. I have employed in some way everything I ever studied.

I believe that I found in graduate work, in particular, a sense of values that has been indispensable in the stresses and strains of administrative work: a feeling for scholarship as a vocation in its own right; for independence in research, experimentation, and thinking; and for intrinsic satisfactions in study and research regardless of success or failure, approbation or condemnation, in the outcome. When prospects looked most bleak, this sense of the value of the intellectual enterprise and my own confidence in its value made it possible for me to trust my own commitment to it and to keep on trying to find and make a place where I could participate happily in it. On the whole, I have found these over and over again in a variety of places and positions, in all of which I have been happy and in all of which I have learned something from both successes and failures. Like Saint Teresa, I am grateful to know that there is useful work for me to do, and if it does not find me, I have only to go out and look for it.

Erica Olson

I was born in Portland, Oregon, in 1923, and raised in East Lansing, Michigan, where my father was a professor of English at Michigan State University. My mother had taught history in high school before her marriage and in college after World War II to help out in an inflated enrollment situation. Other relatives, including my maternal grandmother, an uncle, and a cousin, had also earned graduate degrees and engaged in college teaching. My parents took it for granted that I would get all the education I was entitled to by virtue of my abilities and then put it to work.

Ever since I was quite small it was clear that my principal talents were in the field of music. I consider myself lucky that I knew from childhood that this was the line which I wanted to pursue and that I was encouraged in this by my parents as well as, later, by my teachers. By the time I was ready for college, I had decided to utilize my musical talent by following my father in the field of university teaching and combining it with research, writing, composing, performing, and translating.

Wisely, however, my family insisted on my having a broad liberal education rather than just training in music. Therefore, when I entered Michigan State University in 1936, I decided to major in French and to take just those music subjects which I desired. I was not yet 13 years old at that time and I probably would not have been allowed to start college so early had not my father been on the faculty.

My varied undergraduate courses certainly stood me in good stead at graduate school, where my good preparation in languages, French and German especially, really was a "plus." Although my science studies (pursued pretty intensively as an undergraduate) have not helped me professionally, they have contributed to my enjoyment of life, enabling me to feel a part of nature rather than hostile to it.

I received my B.A. at the age of 16 and for the next two years I attended the University of California at Los Angeles and received an A.M. in music in 1941. I then enrolled as a student in the music department at Columbia and received a Ph.D. when I was 22. My graduate work was financed by scholarships and fellowships with supplementary help from my family. While in New York, I also studied composition and piano with some of the country's foremost artists. Columbia made it possible for me to finish a book on three composers and that was the real start of my career. What a thrill to see the German translation displayed in shop windows in Vienna when I was there in 1960!

When I finished at Columbia I would have loved to have gone on and taught there as many of my male fellow students subsequently did. I was told I could not because I was a woman. This hurt me very much. I also found that teachers at Columbia did not give me much of a professional helping hand after my departure. I have tried not to make this error with my students, for I feel the teacher's concern must extend beyond graduation. However, it was through the Columbia employment bureau that I got my first position as an instructor at Western Maryland College. Despite my youth I experienced no difficulties, and I was fortunate because that position led to the others I have had since. I was also fortunate in that I was able to consult with my family about alternative jobs, since both my parents were experienced in the university field and in a position to be helpful in weighing the relative advantages or disadvantages of different moves.

I was promoted to assistant professor the year after I was hired and I remained at Western Maryland for 4 years. In 1950 I was offered an appointment as assistant professor at Syracuse University and since I considered it a better opportunity from the standpoint of salary and the size and prestige of the school, I accepted. I left this position after 2 years for various reasons: the classes were too large, interfering colleagues irritated me to the extent of affecting my work efficiency in and out of school, and there was an adverse effect on my health due to the climate.

That same year I received a Fulbright research fellowship to collect material in Austria for a book which was eventually published in 1961. While on the fellowship, I made goodwill tours to United States information centers in Austria as a lecturer and performer. Had it not been for the war, I would have been able to visit Austria sooner. This meant that I wrote my book which centers in Vienna without ever having seen the place! However, on the balance maybe that is a good thing.

On my return to this country I was invited by the president of Drew University to start a music department according to my own ideas. I had known him since 1945 when I worked for him at Western Maryland. Therefore, knowing his attitudes, I welcomed this opportunity, particularly since the location was near New York. Since 1959, I have been a full professor of music, as well as department chairman, at this school.

My present position has contributed to my development in making me a better administrator and has given me much freedom to work on my own and with small groups of students. Furthermore, teaching courses in contemporary music has helped me to continually enrich my background in this vital subject which is the heart of my interests. I expect continued growth in the coming few years with additional prestige from publications, performances of my music, and all that goes with these. I also review records and concerts for periodicals; I translate books, and I am a consultant on religious music. The better my work becomes known, the more assignments of various sorts I receive.

I now devote 12 hours a week to teaching, 10 hours to professional organizational work as a board member of various organizations of musicians, and inestimable hours in research, writing, translation, composing, and performing. Fortunately, the favorable conditions of my employment create a situation whereby it is possible to carry out my other work.

As an instructor I am most gratified by teaching an enthusiastic group of music majors who cooperate actively in building up the department. They are fun! I dislike faculty meetings and filling out endless "clock-hour" forms. Frankly, I skip a lot of the red tape to concentrate on what *I* think are the important aspects of my job. There is not as much assistance with messy office detail as you'd find in a larger school. *Too many committees.* (see Parkinson's Law)!

My local volunteer activities have been with community concert and symphony groups. I have enjoyed writing reviews for the local papers and program notes for the orchestras. However, the role of a professional working with non-professionals who do not understand the problems involved can be difficult. My main leisure activity is bird study. I also enjoy reading and collecting mystery novels. All of my outside activities, whether paid or unpaid, have certainly helped on the job by giving me more prestige among colleagues and enabling me to give more richly to my students from my own professional experiences. As of this moment, I have published one book, translated three others, and edited still another. In conjunction with more articles and reviews than can be enumerated, this output has not hurt my promotions!

My parents always assumed that I would concentrate on my career and not be in a hurry to marry. This has proved to be true, although I would not reject the thought of marrying someone in my profession with whom I could work closely. I certainly wish that every capable woman could have the same opportunity to develop all her potentialities that I had. I would have felt cheated if I had not had the chance to build the kind of career I now have. If I should marry I certainly would plan to continue working, although perhaps with a smaller number of classroom hours (I have too many already). I would not plan on children.

My mother's college teaching enabled her to assist me financially when I was just starting to work. This was most helpful. When my parents retired, they moved nearby and when my father died suddenly this year, my home life changed since this left my mother dependent on me for many services (though not financially dependent). As her health worsened, I was no longer able to take care of her, and she is now in a nursing home.

If I hear of an opportunity offering even better financial conditions (both for myself and for the building up of departmental facilities) I might consider leaving my present position. However, it would have to offer me as much or more freedom for my own research and other pursuits as I now have.

Throughout my career I have encountered salary discrimination. This is not admitted in my school, but the pattern is

very clear. As a man I would make at least $1,000 more yearly
—here or elsewhere. If I were to apply for a directorship or a
deanship of a school of music—which I could do very well—I
would (in fact have) run into like obstacles. Just this year,
there occurred a vacancy when one of my former teachers
died. I have not applied since I know I would not even be
considered.

I do feel deeply that sex segregation in our colleges, both of
students and faculty, is as harmful to the total experience of
the student as racial segregation is said to be. I wish to see the
day when I could be invited to teach at Columbia or Yale or
Princeton as a matter of course, without special fuss being
made about it, just because those schools thought that my
qualifications were what they wanted. I know that I have
something unique to offer and I would like to see the best possible use made of my potentialities. While my present post has
many fine features, it does not *completely* make the best use of
what I have to give.

I expect to retire at 65 and to continue with my own research and composing and to visit and work with friends and
colleagues abroad. In the meantime, I have exactly the kind of
career for which I prepared. It has progressed in a pretty
straight line and thus far I have been able to meet the deadlines
which I have set for myself in reaching certain goals. As time
goes on I hope to find even deeper satisfaction in my work, to
overcome its few unsatisfactory features, and to enhance those
which make it not just "work" but an enjoyable way of life.

Cecile Tannenbaum

My father was an Hungarian-born real estate broker who in
1932 lost the job he had held since 1920 and spent the next 6
years desperately trying every type of self-employment (sell-

ing insurance, starting tiny businesses, and so on) before he again obtained a regular job, with the federal government. The effect of my parents' poverty and striving for me is obvious. It was important for me to study and work hard to escape from their social and economic status. As typical poor, semi-educated Jews with a tremendous ambition for my sister and me to be educated and to "succeed," they wanted as much education for me as was possible and I agreed.

I was born in the Bronx in 1923 and attended Hunter College from 1939 to 1943. I had considered being a lawyer since childhood, but I thought for a while that I would first do graduate work in economics, my undergraduate major. However, I recognized that I had very little interest in the statistics and mathematics that would be involved in economics so, by the time I graduated from college, I had decided to go right to law school despite the offer of a fellowship in economics, since I never had any doubts that law was my primary goal. My parents would have preferred that I be a teacher or a doctor (more security), but they didn't fight too much about my going into law.

I received a scholarship to the Columbia Law School which I entered in 1943, planning to prepare for the practice of labor law. I was in a wartime accelerated program and received my LL.B. two years later. While at law school, I was a member of the staff of the Law Review. By graduation, my interest had changed from labor law specialization to the practice of law generally.

I wasn't the type to do much anticipating or long-range planning as a student. I'm much too practical and rooted in the present moment. However, I always assumed that my education and career would come before marriage. Also, but not very consciously, I thought that I'd marry late, if at all, because I had been so involved in my studies that I had very little social life until late in law school. World War II may have affected this by eliminating the men at law school and thereby eliminating distraction. I married at 23!

My husband is also a lawyer and a partner in a law firm. The year before our marriage, and after my graduation from law school, I worked as a legal assistant for a very distinguished New York firm which I knew would provide me with the best possible training. I left the following year because I found there was no future there beyond research, since I was a woman and had no business to bring in. After marriage, I went to a large Western city where my husband practiced, and I entered government service there, which seemed to offer better opportunities for a woman. I became a special assistant to the district attorney until 1950, when I was offered a position as assistant counsel with a newly organized state planning agency that offered more permanency, more experience as one of only four lawyers in the office, and wide litigation opportunity.

I took this in preference to a good offer from a private firm because I believe the government offers a better future for a woman. Most private firms won't allow a woman to do active litigation or to become a partner except in very narrow fields, such as trusts and estates or domestic relations, if they hire her at all. However, once she gets into litigation, a woman is so conspicuous that she moves faster. Four years later I was promoted to associate counsel and handled the most important appeals. I left in 1958, since I felt I had had enough years of arguing cases in a fairly narrow area and wanted more rounded appellate experience. I became an assistant attorney general.

However, I found that even general appellate work was too narrow and left when I was appointed to my present position as general counsel to a city planning agency, where I am in charge of sixty-four lawyers and earn $15,000 a year. I've never run a big law office before, and I'm enjoying the sheer "status" of the job. There are some difficulties with superiors who have never had training in the law—and I'm still unhappy about the narrowness of the law we administer, even as expanded by the various challenges of being chief counsel. I'd leave without any hesitancy if I got a more interesting offer, since I've returned to this field of law only because the opportunities here are so much better than my previous ones.

I spend time outside my work on activities connected with bar associations, civil liberties and political organizations, and the law school alumni. I think such activities are my duty to society, as well as a means to self-expression and career advancement. I enjoy many of them as social outlets but some— oh, the long, boring evenings! For sheer fun, I spend time as an art spectator, listening to music, attending theater, and traveling abroad.

The question of a career is strictly up to the individual woman; she must decide if it means enough to her and if she's willing to face the problems it involves. If she marries, an encouraging husband is vital. My husband has always encouraged my career in every way; he has emphasized my freedom to choose and my abilities, and he has generally made me feel his pride in me. My parents would have liked me to have children and stay at home (as my sister did) or else get a nice secure civil service job (I'm an exempt semi-political appointee); basically, however, my mother particularly got tremendous satisfaction from my career and general freedom and, most fortunately, my husband agrees with my goals and considers both our careers more important than having children. Mainly because of him and my parents, who believed in my education and a career for me, I have hardly ever had any problems in relation to being a woman. I really never was forced to think seriously, let alone worry, about the whole problem of women's rights, and consequently it has seldom concerned me.

Florence Usher

A philosophy professor at college helped me to rationalize my need for excellence and to integrate this with my need to assist the Negro community, of which I am a member. He, and a secondary school teacher who made me aware of my potential, were key influences in my life. In addition, my early education, which was in a progressive elementary school, led me toward an individual and individual-oriented profession. It also contributed to a skepticism which moved me toward science rather than a field more dependent on dogma.

All of the women in my family worked. It was expected that I would. Both of my parents were professionals and this influenced my choice to take up a professional occupation, especially since the limitations of a non-professional life appeared substantial. However, family finances and my parents' relationship, which was difficult, led me to choose a profession different from either of theirs. My mother, who had earned her master's degree, was a school teacher. She returned to teaching when I was in grade school and continued for many years. My father was a clergyman who had two graduate degrees, as well as an honorary one. He shared the view that women should do whatever work they were equipped to do and gave me faith in myself, determination, and moral support.

I was born in Philadelphia in 1919, the second of three children, and I grew up in Chicago. My older sister, who died a few years ago, was an architect, and my younger brother is an engineer. I entered Swarthmore College in 1936, and transferred the following year to Vassar, where I majored in psychology with the goal of becoming a psychologist. By the end of my undergraduate years, I had changed my goal to psychiatry, because I recognized the limitations inherent in the practice of clinical psychology if one is not research-oriented. Moreover, psychology has status limitations and, therewith, limitations of influence. I was urged to consider other possibilities, but rejected them because they were not really attractive to me. Other fields which I considered had other limitations, either in terms of social contribution, e.g., the field of languages, or in terms of intellectual challenge, e.g., obstetrics.

When I was in college, I was not particularly adept at sciences; rather, I found success much easier in other fields. Since mathematics had always been difficult for me, I was afraid of physics, quantitative chemistry, and so on. Not until I was a senior at college did I realize that in spite of all this, I really wanted more than anything to go into medicine. Therefore, I had to spend time after college getting the pre-med courses I had failed to take as an undergraduate. Since I married immediately after graduation, I could not depend on my family for financial support. I had to work to finance my night courses and to save money for medical school tuition.

My husband, who had one year of college, was a statistical clerk and later an accountant in New York. For the few years after I graduated from college, I worked in that city, first in various clerical jobs and later as a biochemical technician, in order to acquire the money I needed. The latter position was the only one which provided not only a salary but also interesting work. By 1943 I was ready to enter medical school, but my applications to three New York City schools were rejected. Because of my husband's work, I was limited to institutions in New York. Fortunately, I was finally admitted to one of them, the College of Physicians and Surgeons, in 1944. These rejections of my applications to medical school are the only evidence of sex discrimination that I have encountered. It was probably World War II and the shortage of male applicants which finally secured my admission, for a woman, 25 years old, married, and out of college 4 years had a better

chance then than at other times. Being a Negro may have
hindered my career in spots, but it has aided it in others.

I entered medical school with the intention of becoming a
psychiatrist and psychoanalyst. I have found that my shift in
goals from psychology to psychiatry was justified, since I have
observed that the very limitations I anticipated in applying
psychological training in a therapeutic way do indeed exist.
My 4 years of work experience between college and medical
school helped me to mature: I became more realistic about
what is necessary to achieve one's goals. My family's influence
was primarily responsible for providing the motivation and
support in my pursuit of a professional career. My father
helped me to attend medical school by permitting us to live
with him at this time.

I gave birth to my only child during the winter of my last
year in medical school and received my M.D. the following
spring. I then served a rotating internship at a city hospital for
a year, followed by 2-year residency in psychiatry at a state
mental hospital. It was here that I started my training in
psychoanalytic medicine, because I knew that theoretical and
technical knowledge in these fields was essential to the most
effective practice of psychological treatment. While undergo-
ing psychoanalytic training, I worked part-time at various
mental health clinics as a therapist. In one instance, I had the
opportunity of establishing a clinic and serving as clinical director until I was replaced by a child psychiatrist. In 1952 I
opened a private practice in addition to my part-time clinic
consulting, and in 1954 I completed my training and received a
certificate as a psychoanalyst.

Five years later I was appointed associate attending psychiatrist at a large hospital where I engaged in part-time hospital
practice and clinic work, for which I was paid $6,800 a year. I
continued in private practice until 1961, when I became director of the department of psychiatry at a public hospital, at a

salary of $25,000 a year. This was an opportunity I had always wanted. I derive great satisfaction from having developed a planned service and making it operate as well as possible. Only the mechanical part of administration is bothersome. I can conceive of changing positions only if I were physically unable to perform my work.

I knew that my husband was not intellectually or professionally oriented and that my work would impose strains on our marriage. I thought it would survive. I was wrong. We were divorced in 1955. This divorce caused me very little emotional strain and had no effect at all on my work. I was remarried two years later to a journalist. My second marriage is a good one in all respects. My husband has never opposed my career activities. I get pleasure from providing an esthetically pleasing and physically comfortable home for my family and me but the effort required to do so produces a great amount of fatigue.

My child's needs were always taken into consideration in choice of work schedules, places of work, and work demands. My ability to work has depended on available household assistance, but this has never been a problem, so my decisions have not been affected by it.

I don't find much time to engage in volunteer activity, but I am a member of several organizations which I consider professional, civic, and social obligations. I am also a member of Phi Beta Kappa and Alpha Omega Alpha, its medical counterpart. I estimate that I spend about 3 to 6 hours a week attending meetings of psychiatric associations, clinic boards, and such. My work, to which I generally devote 50 to 60 hours weekly, is of primary importance in shaping my pursuits. In addition, I estimate that I spend 2 to 4 hours weekly in studying and 10 to 20 in homemaking. I also occasionally attend the theatre and concerts. I anticipate spending even more time in the future on public duties as hospital department head, such as making speeches, public appearances, and attending official functions.

Of the women who went to college with me and had the capacity for graduate study, those who went on seem more satisified than those who didn't. Their families do not appear to have suffered in major ways, though I am sure that there is a physical toll on a working mother which is very real.

As I look back upon all this, I can comment on several factors which seem to have been necessary in achieving the educational and professional levels which I did attain. The first is a very clear, very strong motivation toward a *definite goal* which in itself is relatively *conflict-free*. Possibly only when the above situation exists is a woman able to tolerate or resolve the personal conflicts involved in pursuing advanced education and responsible employment. The second factor is a capacity for persistence and problem-solving. The third is a reasonable amount of *good luck*, and the fourth, strong support from one or more important figures in the family or close environment. This can take many forms—pride in your achievements, guidance, moral support, or financial assistance.

Some or all of these factors must be present to allow any individual to achieve maximally, but they are perhaps even more essential to the optimal development and achievement of the intellectually gifted women in our society and culture at the present time.

THE FAMILY-ORIENTED

There are several reasons why women decide to pursue graduate education. The career-oriented planners are primarily interested in maximizing their skills so that they will be in preferred positions to realize their work aspirations. Other women attend graduate school to prepare for careers, but they do not anticipate that work will be central to their lives. Rather, they expect it to be contingent upon their circumstances. They seek marriage and a family and would prefer to work only prior to the assumption of homemaking responsibilities and, possibly, after these need no longer be their exclusive concern.

There are also women who study beyond the undergraduate level with no aim but that of increasing their intellectual development as a means of attracting educated husbands. When they find that the process of acquiring information is enjoyable and meaningful, they see no reason to cut off their pursuit of more education. The acquisition of career-connected skills is incidental and they are really marking time until marriage.

The high intelligence and superior academic performance of the women in our group permitted them to take advantage of available educational opportunities regardless of their motives for doing so. Although their graduate education set them apart from most women, the values of those who gave priority to family concerns placed them in a more traditional mold. They were first and foremost family oriented. They knew that once they had children, they would willingly surrender their place in the world of work for the gratifications of raising a family and making a home.

Yet, although their values in this respect may be conventional, their education was often utilized beyond the confines of their homes. These women have frequently assumed leadership positions in their communities, where they have been able to satisfy their own needs for intellectual stimulation, as well as their neighbors' need for skilled volunteers. It should be pointed out that, although the two portraits that follow are of women whose graduate education was in the field of social work, the family-oriented planner is found in almost every field. The desire to serve one's family and one's neighbors is of course not the exclusive characteristic of one particular profession.

With the passage of time, the growth of their children has served to influence many women in this group to consider new plans for the future. For most of them, their education has already proved to be an asset in their roles as wives and mothers. They are now in a preferred position to enter or reenter the labor market because they had the foresight to acquire specialized training early.

Harriet Coleman

My parents were native Chicagoans; I was born in Chicago in 1922 and lived there until I graduated from college. My father, who had no education beyond grade school, was a railroad machinist during the early years of my life. He loved cars, so he left his job during the Depression to be a foreman in a big downtown garage. He was laid off in the mid-thirties and I remember one miserable year when he worked in an icehouse, then sold vacuum cleaners. We had no heat, and little food. My father later returned to his railroad job.

My mother was a high school graduate who had no work experience until the 1940s when I was a college student. At that time there was nobody home, nothing to do, and debts to repay, so she took a job as a saleswoman in a department store. She enjoyed seeing people and got personal satisfaction from being an efficient worker. She worked steadily thereafter until her retirement about four years ago. I have one older brother who is now a salesman.

I was very withdrawn during my adolescence and my mother pushed me into the Girl Reserves, a teen-age group centered at the YMCA. There I "came out of it," and often

assumed leadership. The group had an adviser who, I later realized, must have been a trained social worker. My relationship
with her had a quality of closeness and empathy which I had
never before experienced and which was extremely helpful. I
realize in retrospect that I probably quite unconsciously
wanted to be like her.

As a result, when I entered the University of Chicago in
1941, I decided to major in sociology in order to prepare myself for a career in social work. My family was surprised by
my decision to go to college. In fact, they objected, but I went
anyway. Later, they were proud of my achievements and had
no objection to my going on to graduate school, although they
thought I was "a little crazy" to go into social work, even
though they thought it would be "interesting." Yet, the fact
that they and I have very little ambition to acquire a great deal
of money made a career which doesn't pay much quite a natural choice, despite the difficult economic and emotional aspects
of my family life. In addition, my parents' generally cooperative attitudes also influenced my selection of a career.

I worked my way through college except for about $400
that my mother gave me from her earnings. After graduation in
1944, I thought of joining the WAVES, but my father objected. Therefore, I followed my parents to Texas where they
had moved and took a job as a social worker in the only
agency in town. After a year, because I wished to leave home,
I left to go to Dallas, where I took the best available job opportunity as an interviewer for an urban renewal agency. I kept
this one year, then took a job with the public welfare department, since it seemed to involve real social work.

Two years later, in 1948, I left this position to enter the
New York School of Social Work, for I had become aware,
via contacts with professionally trained social workers during
my 4 years of employment, that I was not really a professional.
I chose to study casework (rather than group work or re-

search) since that is probably the most *basic* of the fields of
social work. Without fellowship and scholarship aid, I would
have had to spend additional years working and saving in order
to attend graduate school. I also made additional money by
working as a medical social worker at Columbia Presbyterian
Medical Center during the summer between my 2 graduate
school years. I took my training there during my second graduate year, and they wanted me to stay permanently. This was
an attractive opportunity, but I wanted to be closer to my
parents.

My graduate school experience gave me a very good picture
of what working as a professional in my field would really be
like. It has been very much as expected—complex! Most gratifying is the creative use of one's whole personality, which is
also the most difficult aspect. I have found that I need considerable satisfaction in personal relationships in order to work
happily. If this were missing, I might prefer a less demanding
field.

After receiving my master's degree in 1950, I returned to
Dallas and took a job as a social worker at a county hospital
while awaiting an appointment at an army hospital. I received
the appointment the following year, and worked there as a
medical social worker for 2 years. I had many marriage opportunities which I did not follow up until I met my husband-to-
be at the hospital. We were married in 1952 when I was 30. He
is a physician and when he left the army to set up practice in a
small Texas town, I accompanied him to our present home
and became a caseworker for the county social welfare
agency. I would gladly have fled back to Dallas six months
after we got here. *No* plays, *no* museums, *no* interesting
shops!! And now we're here forever. Once a doctor establishes
a practice, he stays in one place. A year later, I was asked to
become chief social worker for the county health department
and, although I had qualified to become a supervisor at a

higher salary for my former employer, I accepted this position
because I was unwilling to stay in a backward agency. I left
this position in 1956 to have a baby. My final salary was somewhere in the neighborhood of $500 a month.

I believe that I held an unvoiced conviction that a married
woman should, if she likes, continue a career after marriage
until the arrival of children. Since the birth of my daughter, I
have remained at home. When she was about a year old, I was
asked to work half-time on a research project for the county. I
don't like housework and being alone, so I considered it. But I
imagined how concerned I would be to be away from the
baby every day, so I knew I could never take the job.

As a homemaker, I enjoy watching and helping the development of my child and helping my husband in his career.
Decorating and gardening also interest me, and I want to do
things with the house, but can't because my husband thinks it's
unnecessary. I could insist, but my training makes it hard for
me to do this. I find I have a greater need than ever to just *be
with people*, but again my husband's tastes interfere, though
we do play bridge and dominoes with friends.

Since moving here, I have devoted about 6 hours a week to
various community organizations. These include activities related to the Unitarian Church, the Democratic party, housing,
youth, family service, YWCA, music, medical auxiliaries, and a
cooperative nursery school. I participated in these because I
was asked and because none was foreign to my basic convictions. In some cases, I helped to start new agencies, and twice I
engaged in research for local government agencies. I live in an
underdeveloped area, and it's been fun to help get some things
rolling. Yet, volunteer activity is an unsatisfactory substitute
for a job in my field. I dislike the lack of continuity, the cas-
ualness of approach of many co-workers, and the apparent social emphasis often shown when the sole purpose of a meeting
seems to be to have lunch.

If I had no children, I'd be working, very probably at my most recent job as a chief social worker for the county health department. Next fall, my child starts kindergarten. It is unlikely I will have another child, and I have begun to ponder what I shall do with my time while she's away at school. I *do* think children need their mother at home, except for school hours. Though he has a say in other areas, my husband leaves any decisions regarding work up to me. However, he has recently been appointed as county commissioner of health, and this may affect my work decision if a conflict of interest is concerned.

There is no question that my education largely determines the nature of my spare-time activities; it contributed greatly to my attitudes toward my child, relatives, and friends. It may have been part of my appeal for my husband! Yet, if I were 18 again, I would go to school and study the following things: fine cooking and sewing, music, art, literature, philosophy, psychology and the basic sciences. Actually, this is not much different from what I did study, except for the cooking and sewing. But, when I was 18 I could not enjoy it. I had to get finished and go to *work* (influence of the Depression?). Doing it over again, I would want a *real* liberal education, with *no hint* of career about it. *Then*, I would get married and probably have one child (only one, you see, because I agree with Margaret Mead that this is one thing we can do to keep population figures down). When I had met that child's needs, I might or might not want to train for a career—but if I did, I'd probably be in better emotional and financial condition to do it and have more to offer sooner after training to the consumers of my service.

This is a *terribly* complex matter, of course, but I did find myself agreeing with a *Harper's* article which suggested that educational institutions had better start arranging things so that wives and mothers of older children can study more conveniently.

I do feel that I performed very well in my field and was rewarded in many ways. But in terms of the long-lasting effects of the choice on my life as a whole, I have some difficulty calling the choice of field "satisfactory." The term satisfactory does seem to involve happiness. My difficulty in giving an unqualified yes relates to my doubt that my professional training contributed to my level of happiness. The training itself was (and I believe typically is) a *painful* experience. Practice after a year or so brought self-understanding and proficiency, and professional experience became relatively pleasant. The aspect of it which remains upsetting is this: One loses one's illusions quite completely, and in trying to live an ordinary life (as a housewife, for example) it is hard to get along without them! It is hard to *be* an ordinary person with the knowledge and attitudes acquired in training in social work. I almost believe that this *particular* career ought not be mixed with having a family; that is, that perhaps for women it is one of the more difficult professions.

Kathryn Greeley

I always assumed that I would get a complete education and work at an interesting job before marriage. Most of my mother's friends had had interesting jobs before they were married or still had them if they were unmarried. I hoped to marry a professor and live exactly the life my parents had!

My father was a professor of Spanish at Western Reserve University. I was born in Cleveland in 1923 and was brought up in a suburb of that city. Both of my parents were native Midwesterners. My mother had completed two years of college, and before her marriage at the age of 35, she was a librarian. She stopped working after she married until I was in high school, when she became director of a social welfare association, a position she held until she was 73. She always needed the money, but I think other satisfactions became even more important—the social contacts, ego, usefulness. I had decided to be a social worker before she went back to work, but I was influenced by the knowledge of her interesting career before she was married, of the traveling and many friends and experiences she packed in before settling down to marriage at a comparatively late age. I assumed that I would be at least 30 before I would marry.

Everything was geared to leading me toward college degrees and a career. I had to go to my father's college and get scholarships because there was no spare money, but otherwise everything was easy and smooth. My parents' life was so pleasant, with vacations, parties, and good conversation, that I wanted the same. My younger sister probably rebelled against my pattern; she did not study hard, and completed only one year of college. She had a series of jobs she didn't like and married at the age of 25. Her husband is a psychiatrist, and they and their three small children live in a university setting where her activities center about the home. Yet, my sister seems as educated as I do in any group.

I don't know what I read when I was very young which gave me the idea that I would become the lovely lady with a basket bringing crumbs and gracious living to the grateful poor. In any event, from the time I entered college in 1941, I had one goal—to be a social group worker of the Jane Addams type in poor neighborhoods. Everyone advised me to take a well-rounded general course in college and to specialize in graduate school. Since I never wavered in my intention to be a social worker, everyone agreed that I should be trained for better jobs and salaries. Therefore, I had no real undergraduate major, but concentrated on social sciences and French. World War II may have kept me from meeting a possible husband during college—thank goodness.

During my college years, I worked with groups of children at settlement house day camps every summer plus two afternoons a week during the winters. I enjoyed this work and was considered good at it. It confirmed me in my certainty that group work was right for me. Thus, when I entered the New York School of Social Work in 1945, I planned to specialize in that area of social work. In fact, after six months of casework, my advisors and I agreed that I should be back in group work. I did take a variety of courses and was interested in, but scared by, community organization as a specialty. Group work seemed right for me. My good grades and my extracurricular activities in college got me a full scholarship for my year of graduate school. My mother's best friend gave me a scholarship the second year.

After receiving my master's degree in 1947, I was employed as a group worker by a New York YM–YWHA. I had been a social work student there, loved it, and wanted another year of sheltered supervision. It was a one-year job and I knew I had to return home the following year because of my father's illness. In Cleveland, I took the best job available at a YWCA as teen-age program director. After a while, I got a "nervous stomach" from the responsibility involved in my job, and I didn't feel very useful there anyhow. I didn't like the working hours, which kept me from meeting men—since I wanted to find a husband. When I was in graduate school, it never occurred to me to consider any problems in combining marriage and a career. After all, my mother had held interesting jobs without disrupting our family life. I figured that if the right man didn't come along, I would be happiest working with children, spending evenings with groups that needed me. To my surprise, I began to resent the evenings and weekends at work, as they kept me from dates and parties. Like many of my friends, I was about ready to find a more reasonable job, but luckily the right man came along and rescued me.

In 1950, I had the opportunity to spend a year in France as a visiting group worker. It meant adventure and the chance to live and talk nothing but French. It was great! I arranged for the year in France, figuring that, after that, I would be ready to take up filing or scrubbing floors. Luckily, I met my husband before I left for France. He was a medical student and we became engaged before I left and planned to marry when I returned. Six months later, after I had worked in five different locations in France, the Korean crisis made my fiancé suddenly draft-eligible. Therefore, I came back to the States to be married.

After my marriage in 1951, when I was 28, I went to Denver with my husband, who was about to begin his internship. I worked as a professional worker for the Girl Scouts for one month until my husband was drafted into the Public Health Service. He spent 3 years in the Indian Service as a general practitioner rather than specializing; it was an interesting experience for us to live on reservations. Since then, except for a recent 2-month stint as a substitute French teacher in public school, I have been at home. I took the teaching job because I was dying to try it, since I had experimented in giving private lessons. Since I have had my own children, I have felt no interest whatever in resuming my career as a group worker. As a matter of fact, I have been moderately bored by my occasional involvement as a leader of scouting groups, such as the Campfire Girls and the Brownies.

I now have three children, aged 10, 9, and 7. My husband teaches pharmacology at a southern medical school, and we live in a faculty housing development which is wonderful, since it makes it possible to leave children with good neighbors and friends. I have been very active in community volunteer projects and my main activity at the moment is as a member of the state board and as chairman of the Local Job Committee of the Council of Human Relations, which is involved in interracial affairs of the Urban League type. I am also currently a member of the League of Women Voters and of the PTA, and I worked actively in the Kennedy campaign. I estimate that I spend 15 hours a week in volunteer activities; interracial work is my deepest interest.

I start out in voluntary pursuits because I believe in them. I stay if I find a useful niche or if I meet interesting people, or both. They often give life more meaning. Neighbors got us involved in the interracial Council of Human Relations, and now we have so many Negro friends and such personal concern for their disadvantaged position that we read and talk and push for integration (or hold our tongues and bide our time, but never lose awareness) all the time, and so do our friends. This means impromptu interviews, conversations as well as committee work, and other related activities. My husband and I together have taken on the presidency of the local Council of Human Relations for next year, knowing that this may double and triple the time we already spend on it. I am so glad I don't have a job right now! This is "community organization" really, the third branch of social work, though the idea of doing it full-time would terrify me.

My husband approves of my activities and job ventures—his mother always worked. He helps with the children and cooking and he also comes to meetings. The children are really independent. We have a good reciprocal baby-sitting arrangement with neighbors. (I have a cleaning woman 3½ hours a week.) I think it is good for kids to see their parents involved in community life. All three are happy and doing well in school. We are selfish enough to consider only ourselves and choose to live far from both of our families. There's lots of visiting back and forth but it doesn't influence our lives basically.

I am so glad that I have the right husband and a home and children that I really enjoy all the tasks like dishes and diapers which help me feel that I am earning some of my good luck. Since my husband loves to cook, does not mind a messy house, and enjoys bringing up the children with me, it becomes obvious that I am not a good sport but rather that I have a soft, good deal. He enjoys entertaining and going to parties and concerts. We read books and articles and discuss them together. We go camping with our children in the summer. We have friends and relatives as house guests. My friends remind me often, "I hope you know how lucky you are."

I often wonder what my education has contributed to my life. I hope all those courses in college and graduate school made me better educated and more interesting. I feel competent and happy in the university atmosphere we live in, but so does my sister with one year of college! Actually, I question the exact value of my college and graduate school education (aside from making me eligible for jobs). It was logical for me to go right along from college to graduate school and on to jobs, and I am very glad I accomplished all this before I was married. I think I enjoy my retirement into motherhood and housework much more because I lived long enough as a single woman. Now I think I am better prepared to look around at possible future careers than most of my friends.

I would like to think that my master's degree is helpful in community work, but I am afraid that I work and think in the same way as I did in similar organizations in college. I think that any wisdom or insight or skill comes more from experience than schooling. This is subversive thinking, I realize, and is the kind of thing I usually confide only to my husband.

As a student, everything was open to me. I never considered

teaching or nursing, though I hope my daughters will choose them rather than social work. (Better hours, easier to take advantage of part-time temporary openings without such long-term commitment.) I graduated from idealization of social work to realistic play-ground work in settlement houses and learned the "right" attitudes in school and from professional social workers. I don't know why my mind was so closed to other vocations. My husband says he chose medicine in the same blind determined way and is just lucky he happened to like it. I have no regrets because it all has turned out nicely. But I still need to be needed.

I don't know how I could have done things differently. I felt no doubts at any time. Now, I don't want to be a group worker as I knew the work before marriage, but probably my training was a good springboard for whatever careers into which fate and my initiative might lead me.

Right now I'm glad to be safe at home with family and community work. But jobs make me feel alive and important and needed and useful. In social work I do not like the pressure of meeting deadlines, mustering up audiences and volunteers, and recording minute details. I have really disliked jobs where I wondered if I was really needed. As our children get older, I will spend more time in community activities or will consider a job, as I have been gradually doing for the past 3 years. It looks as though I might change to teaching French. My "group work personality" is indispensable and I adore having a "captive audience." French has been my indulgence until now—I never thought of it professionally before. But I volunteered with my children's classes last year, and the regular French teacher suggested me as her replacement. Otherwise, I would never have dreamed of it. I may take some courses to help me teach the subject—maybe.

But since I don't want to go into my old field of group work, and since my taste of casework was not alluring, I may

find that my training is somewhat wasted. Certainly, if I were
to seek graduate training now it would not be what I sought
seventeen years ago. This makes me wonder whether women
should divide their education into eras, with specialized training saved for their more mature years after their children are
raised. Perhaps we should be encouraged to work for a few
years after receiving a B.A. degree so as to know better what
our field should be and to have more experience to bring to it.
In my own case, I followed the "best" advice to advance prop-
erly up the social work ladder. So the "proper" advice would
have to change, with apprenticeships offered and encouraged
for potential career girls, but graduate school withheld for several years.

Most women get restless after their children go off to school
and seem to need something to fill their lives with interest and
a feeling of being important. (Housework and gardening and
PTA and church work and entertaining do fill the gap for
many, at least while the children's illnesses and household
emergencies occur unpredictably enough to keep us feeling
like busy mothers.) But most of us seem to turn a corner and
find ourselves ready to be involved in the world again. I know
so many women who love to go off to work every day and
whose children are not hurt that I certainly am in favor of
married women working when they need to and want to. In
my own case, I am grateful that I can venture forth slowly and
try this and that with no financial pressure. Most of my friends
and neighbors are frankly envious of my master's degree which
helps me receive job offers with fairly decent pay from time to
time. Even though my field was social work, my M.S.W. was
counted in determining my salary as substitute teacher. It gives
me confidence that I am worth something.

Perhaps my present thinking about women and careers and
marriage and graduate work is most truly revealed when I try
to put it into advice to my daughters (aged 7 and 10, but it is

never too early to start giving advice!). I would say: If possible, don't meet the right man to marry until you have packed in plenty of school, and travel, and men, and jobs, and living. Try to find some interesting career to ride on—it will lead to more interesting jobs, travels, men, and so on. Nursing has an advantage over social work and teaching after you are married, because you can always take part-time work at odd times of your choosing. The other two usually involve contracts for a year with long-term responsibility plus the obligation, if possible, to stay 2 or 3 years at least in the same job.

College usually opens more interesting jobs to you; Aunt Connie never liked the jobs she could get with only one year of college. On the other hand, if something fascinating comes along which puts off college, don't worry—Aunt Connie is as educated as I am for her life with a doctor husband and three children and seems just as happy. As time goes on, though, she may become dissatisfied and go back to college and graduate school as other friends have done—and maybe she will pick a career she likes better than I do social work. Maybe I will be in graduate school learning a new trade at the same time!

The most important goal is meet enough men so that you will find the right one and not settle for anything less along the way. Maybe he won't come along, but if you keep doing interesting things the odds are with you, so have faith. Before you settle down pursue many interests so you won't bog down with babies and housework. Be sure you and your husband have plenty of mutual interest in outside things instead of just concentrating on each other—it makes life more purposeful and fun. It is better for kids not to have their mother absorbed in domestic life and the children. (They agree on this even when they have to do the dishes as I rush off to a meeting. We enjoy the next peaceful evening together all the more!)

If you can muster up some interest in scientific subjects, by all means major in science, for there will be so many men in that field (as opposed to teaching, library work, social work, and so on). But don't rush to marry any of them. If you marry too young, you will always wonder what you missed. But probably you will enjoy the traditional women's fields more and you certainly should enjoy whatever work you do. This means training, usually in school. Otherwise, you will end up being a secretary or salesgirl, and that gets boring.

This advice sounds more like Ann Landers than a vocational guidance counselor. I seem to sound superficial about careers when I place them below other items, but I'm being honest. I am busy enjoying an admittedly pleasant stage of family life when all goes smoothly and all things in the future look possible. Obviously, I am in the same exploratory stage as this survey in which I am taking part, which seems amazingly well-timed for me. Ask me 10 years from now and I may sing a different tune.

THE WORKING MOTHERS

The outstanding characteristic of the planners who are working mothers is that they plan their lives so that they will be able to have both families and careers. It is not accidental that these women have combined these two facets of their lives. This was their conception of their future lives and they have accomplished their goals. A few made long-range plans that allowed for extended careers before they had children, followed by adjustments in their work after motherhood. But regardless of variations in their plans, the significant characteristic of these women is their desire to combine home and work and their success in achieving this goal.

Most of the women in this group have worked more or less

continuously since graduate school. Some have dropped out of
the work force for brief periods after the birth of a child.
Most of them have worked full-time. Others have sometimes
been employed part-time or have engaged in free-lance work.
Although a part-time schedule is more conducive to the discharge of home responsibilities, it does not necessarily result in
a woman's relaxing her desire to realize her career aspirations.

The important point about these working mothers is that
both work and home are important to them. Those who
avoided early marriage were able to acquire experience and
skills that would prove useful when they sought to pursue
their career goals. They were willing to run the risk of postponing marriage, including the risk of not marrying at all.
Others found early marriage to be no barrier to work since, in
most cases, their husbands encouraged and supported their
efforts.

Educated women marry educated men. By virtue of their
own high intellectual interests and standards, educated men are
more likely to prove sympathetic to their wives' needs for careers than are men with less schooling. It is easier for a woman
to span the worlds of home and work if her husband supports
her goals. Often a man is willing to make adjustments in his
own life to permit his wife to better cope with her responsibilities in both worlds.

Many of these women believe that their working enhances
their relationship with their children, who benefit from having
mothers whose satisfactions from their work provide a relaxed
and stimulating atmosphere in the home. If they had to choose
between work and home, these women would have to choose
home, but few have found it necessary to renounce their career goals. Many have made strenuous efforts to tailor the circumstances of their lives to their needs for fulfillment both at
home and at work.

Karen Frank

My family has always acted as if my two sisters and I were boys. They definitely wanted their daughters to be career-oriented. This must have been a large part of the motivating force behind my own career. I had everything going for me; I could have had as much education as I wanted—and more. Within my memory, my parents were always wealthy enough to afford the best, and we had it, in education particularly. They were ambitious for us, both with regard to careers and husbands, though especially with the former I think. There was emphasis on being able to support oneself "just in case." There were certain standards to be kept up.

My parents were immigrants from Eastern Europe with minimal education. My father, who became a successful textile manufacturer, had attended religious school until the age of 13 and my mother had gone through only the fourth grade, but she also had some subsequent training in art. She worked, as a seamstress, only before she married. My sisters and I were raised in Milwaukee, where I was graduated from high school at the age of 17. Today, my sisters are homemakers, but one is now starting to make and sell ceramics, and one is an elementary school teacher.

I attended the University of Wisconsin where I majored in English composition since I had "wanted to write" ever since a high school English teacher required that I drop Zola and read the children's classics first—my first effort of the imagination. However, at the university I discovered I didn't know what to write about, and to teach English at the college level, which I early considered, seemed too conventional a career. By graduation in 1947, I had been steered by a friend of my father toward foreign service and Columbia. I enrolled for the

two-year course at the Columbia School of International
Affairs, since I was underage for the diplomatic service and
also lacked substantive background in economics and political
science.

When I received my master's degree in 1949, one of my
professors pooh-poohed my "book-larnin'" and sent me back
into the world, when I would otherwise have gone on for the
Ph.D. as my father wanted. I applied for entrance into the
Foreign Service and, while awaiting clearance, worked as a
junior writer. A year later, having passed the Foreign Service
exam, I was appointed third secretary of an embassy in Asia.
My job required that I travel considerably through India, Pak-
istan, Burma, Ceylon, and Afghanistan.

I received great help from foreigners whom I met by
chance, presumably because I was a woman and traveling
alone. The Americans were something else again. In fact I feel
I met with prejudice (because of my sex) in every personnel
office where I was interviewed, whether in the Department of
State or later on in large industrial corporations. Many of them
frankly admitted to me they felt that women have no place in
big business or in big jobs. Two years later I was assigned to a
European embassy. I left the service after this tour since I had
previously decided to take only two assignments, because I
was aware that for a woman, foreign service is incompatible
with marriage. Since I did not wish to marry until I was at
least 30, I had to be sure that I was not carried away by the
glamour of the job.

Eventually, I set my sights on teaching, which is not necessarily incompatible with marriage—depending on the man.
English teaching, my original goal, can be a lifetime career for
a woman; foreign service should not be, and I went into it
with a time limit in mind. I enjoyed my service tremendously,
and am very glad I had it; nevertheless I could not recommend
it to any young woman who seeks the usual goal of home and

family. While abroad I received some marriage proposals, and, while there was a certain attraction to a bizarre marriage, I didn't believe myself capable of the sustained effort required to keep one going.

When I terminated my foreign service career, I remained abroad for a year in order to reorient myself before going back to the States. My interest in foreign affairs was by then confirmed, and I continued in a predoctoral program at the London School of Economics with the thought of some day taking a Ph.D. and teaching in this field. While studying I served as an instructor at various U.S. Air Force bases in England.

I returned to Milwaukee in 1956. Although, theoretically, I could have settled anywhere, I wished to be near my parents. I applied broadcast to manufacturing firms, social welfare organizations, international student centers, and chambers of commerce. None of them hired me. I felt there was definitely discrimination against women at a professional level. Some time later I was offered the post of executive assistant at a new school of foreign affairs at an Eastern university, but I declined since I wished to remain in Milwaukee. I do have regrets about not taking this position. I was finally offered a job by a Jewish community organization in an executive capacity. I took it because I could find absolutely no other salaried employment, because many community figures urged me to, and because I thought I ought to meet some people of my own cultural background after having been away so long. I had always been interested in the American Jewish community and the job would permit me to fulfill a desire to travel. However, I found that I didn't like the work and was not suited to organizational employment, so I resigned after 2 years. While I was engaged in this work, I initiated a weekly news column on international affairs which was later syndicated. I continued doing this until 1959, when marriage made it impossible for me to resume traveling and thus keep my information fresh. In 1957 I was invited to teach at the local branch of the University of Wisconsin and have continued to serve as a part-time instructor working as their schedule requires and my pregnancies permit.

My husband is a lawyer and also teaches part-time at Wisconsin. I had one child in 1960 and another 3 years later. My husband and I basically agree that my first care is the children. Beyond that, he offers me the widest possible latitude in choice of occupation. He has often dissuaded me from taking on something that would only dissipate energy, and has been most helpful to me in my writing. I have not had to work for financial reasons, nor do I want to work full-time. Some part-time or temporary jobs were offered to me (to teach, write instructional pamphlets) but I was able to take them only as and if I could get responsible household help. On some occasions, this was the critical factor. This meant, for example, turning down an offer of a permanent contract to teach at Wisconsin. I enjoy watching the children grow and trying to help them avoid mistakes I made.

I was lucky and could have my cake and eat it too only because I was not gripped by the current mania for marrying young, and because I eventually was able to marry a man whose ego doesn't feel threatened either by my past exploits or by my current achievements. Though not a writer himself, he is willing to discuss my writing problems with me, and often is able to steer me through a thought I can't manage myself; when I became ill during the middle of a teaching stint, he finished the term for me. Yet he never considers these activities as anything but auxiliary to our personal relationship. How an active woman would manage without the same kind of husband, I simply don't know.

I am not currently engaged in any volunteer activity because I find it impossible to work on a committee, but I have spoken for some groups, such as the American Field Service, Hebrew schools, career conferences—and enjoy it. I read, write, and play the piano for relaxation, mostly read—it restoreth my soul.

I now teach and write for publication on subjects within the sphere of international affairs. My weekly teaching hours vary from term to term and I spend about 10 hours a week in writing and the rest on homemaking. When I have time, I think about subjects on which to write. I have written a high school text on United States foreign policy and a manual for the American Field Service exchange program, both on commission. I have also written a juvenile European history, about fifty free lance newspaper articles, and four or five articles for national magazines.

I get great satisfaction out of being able to develop and express ideas. Writing and college teaching are admirably suited for this; organizational or bureaucratic hierarchy tended to dampen it for they require the working out of a political *modus vivendi* with colleagues and clients. Hopefully, any change will be far in the future since I am just starting a family. Perhaps, after the children are raised, I will want to work full-time again, but not now. If I decide I would really like a permanent university affiliation, I may work for a Ph.D.

I did what I hoped to do, within biological limitations. That is to say, my male classmates have combined full-time career and family, and I am very much aware of that.

A woman who does not wish to be competitive with men might just as well end her education with high school. Higher education does nothing quite so well as unfit her for housework. If she desires to go and has the capacity for it, I am all for college, career, and "the world" after she has started her children to school. My ideal world would be quite different: It would be one in which women could train for the careers to which they felt suited because, one, suitable ayahs or governesses would be available to help mother the children and, two, men would not feel that work makes women unfeminine. I don't see either of these two things on the horizon in contemporary American society.

Having lived abroad I can compare the status of women here and elsewhere. The Pakistanis, for example, repress their women so badly that those with spunk exert a correspondingly greater effort to do something with their lives. The result is that thousands upon thousands of women are active in fields American women leave alone—politics is an outstanding example, and so is medicine. At the opposite end of the scale, we must look like Pakistanis to the Russians, who were forced to emancipate women because of manpower losses during the war. Perhaps as their population comes into better balance, they too will shove women back into a wholly biological existence. (How would men like to be judged solely by their ability to father children!)

So much depends upon the woman, her job, and her husband. If a woman wants a vocation, can she submerge it in favor of diapers and dishwashing? She probably ought to work (provided her husband can bear it) and pay for competent help out of her salary.

Going a step beyond this, a lot of women are so confused by what society expects or doesn't expect of them that they are unable to function adequately as mothers. A nervous and frustrated mother probably does her child a service by leaving her in the care of paid help. So often the trouble is to find the person to substitute at home. There is no one: The extended family doesn't exist; the maiden aunt has an apartment (and a life) of her own; the grandmother is not wanted. The "maid" is any unskilled worker who can get hired, and often her home background is not one you want to see transferred to your own child.

As mentioned before, two things will have to change before

American women can work out a more useful role for themselves. First, there must be evolved the profession of ayah, housekeeper, governess, or whatever you choose to call her: women who make a career out of running a home and helping to raise children, who are trained for this work, and adequately paid. This would help in two ways: first, by providing a respectable profession for some women who are presently without one and who would not "demean" themselves by working as maids (nor accepting a maid's salary), and, second, by allowing other women to work outside their homes secure in the knowledge that their households and families would not fall apart.

The other prerequisite is even more unlikely to materialize than the one mentioned above. This is a change of attitude on the part of American men so that they no longer require women to submerge their femininity if they desire to hold down jobs. I am well aware of the prevailing stereotype of the successful career woman as masculine. I know how she gets that way. As surely as any other group, women succumb to a self-fulfilling prophecy.

Alexandra Jervis

My parents were of Greek descent. Consequently, our background and interest in ancient culture, our use of the modern Greek language at home, and our trips to Greece when I was a child all led me directly into archaeology.

I was born in Buffalo in 1916, and entered the local university in 1935, where I majored in classics with the intention of becoming an archaeologist and teacher. From the age of 12, when I first visited the remarkably beautiful country of Greece, I knew that I wanted to become an archaeologist. I recall no alternative aspiration except perhaps, at the age of 6, to become

a ballet dancer. But my family encouraged me toward scholarship, and they rigorously forbade interest in a stage career.

My father was a lawyer, a graduate of an American university, and my mother was a graduate of a select girls' school
whose faculty was largely drawn from the University of
Athens. To her everlasting regret she never pursued the teaching career for which she had been prepared, and her restless-
ness around the house made me realize the limitations of domestic activity for an educated mind. Nevertheless, she trained
me as an excellent housewife in an unsparing European tradition and I could successfully run a house when I was 12. At an
early age I decided not to repeat my mother's experience.
Moreover, my parents were very much in favor of my following an academic career.

The year after my graduation in 1939, I worked as an assistant curator of anthropology at the Buffalo Museum of Natural
Science. In 1941 I entered Columbia University in order to do
graduate work in the department of fine arts and archaeology.
My parents had paid for my undergraduate education, but I
insisted on working my way through graduate school, which
was a time-consuming mistake. But perhaps it was necessary in
order for me to mature. Until 1945, when I was made a university fellow, I engaged in various kinds of employment, mostly
as a Latin teacher at two private schools for girls. After receiving my fellowship, I was able to study without undertaking
paid employment. Although my undergraduate training was
poor, my graduate education was the finest, though limited in
range.

At the age of 31 I was married to a man who later became a
professor of English and an outstanding literary critic. I also
began teaching Latin at a private school in Princeton where
my husband and I lived. I taught because I wanted to be self-
supporting while I worked on my dissertation. I received my
Ph.D. in 1952, a few months after my first child was born, and

a year before the birth of my second. We moved to Boston in 1953, and I spent the first year there at home with my children.

After a time I taught Latin, again at the secondary school level, since I needed money to pay for a baby-sitter while I did research in the summer and at other times. The headmistress was difficult and the teaching rather boring, although the students, as always, made it endurable. I left after two years, when I received a postdoctoral research fellowship from the American Association of University Women (AAUW) for travel and study in Greece. I pleaded that I needed the money for baby-sitting help as well as for travel and the committee generously gave me $500 more than I had asked for. On returning, I was appointed lecturer in classics at Brandeis University where my husband was also teaching. My grant as well as scholarly publication seemed to give me the necessary prestige to be considered for a university appointment. Although there was no nepotism ruling as such at the university, no wife of any faculty member had as yet been admitted to the full-time teaching staff. My appointment set a happy precedent.

The following year my husband had a visiting appointment at Wayne State University, and I had one at the University of Michigan. We lived in Ann Arbor. I turned down a permanent appointment there because Brandeis agreed to take me back as assistant professor of classics, and insure my status in the regular ranks. Teaching at the university level is undeniably more satisfying than at the secondary school level. University instruction combines intellectual challenge with the enjoyment of being with lively young people. In addition, there is much pleasure in the stimulating conversation of faculty members of various disciplines. In our home, we had a lively, intellectual, social life, for we entertained extensively, especially people from the Boston and New York literary world.

At that time I spent 9 hours weekly in teaching, about 30

hours in the preparation of lectures and on my own research into the problems of Greek culture, and about 25 hours on homemaking and keeping the family happy. We seemed to do more interesting things together, such as traveling, going to museums, picnicking, exploring local historical sites, and so on, than most families with non-working mothers. The time we had together seemed all the more precious to us. At one brief period I even found myself in the unqualified role of Cub Scout denmother. But I always knew that I was better as a part-time mother than I would be as a full-time mother. Moreover, I felt that the time I spent teaching and learning from other people's children helped me in understanding my own. In any case, staying at home and not exercising my mind for better or for worse would be as debilitating as if I, a normal, healthy person, were to be confined to a wheelchair. The combination of outside work and home work has provided an all-important emotional equilibrium. The balance was best achieved by liter-ally compartmentalizing my life: At home I was entirely do-mestic, at the university I tended to my students exclusively, and for research and writing the library was my haven.

Domestic duties, husband, and children were time-consum-ing, but to see our children grow tall, healthy, attractive, with bright and interested minds, refined sensibilities, and sweet souls as well, seemed like a miracle of gratification. At home I especially liked to cook creatively for appreciative appetites and to furnish a house that reflected our tastes, our travels, and a feeling for tradition and which did not look like a collection of objects purchased from the nearest contemporary furnish-ings store. I hate ironing, cleaning closets, and the like, but I cannot live or think clearly in untidy surroundings. Cleanli-ness, order, and beauty must be attended to, for they are a necessary background for intellectual achievement and emo-tional security.

In spite of the good parts of our marriage, there were unresolved conflicts; my husband and I were separated several years ago, and he moved to California. I found that I was able to stand on my own feet, and achieved the rank of associate professor and tenure at Brandeis. The teaching, research, and the children were sustaining, indeed, in the years following our separation and subsequent divorce. In general our marriage enabled me to keep growing and stimulated and aided my work as well. My husband, a brilliant and creative man, influenced my career by vastly increasing my intellectual understanding and range of interests. I always had faith in myself, but he taught me how to write and behave like a professional.

In addition to marriage and my professional career, one other social factor has been of major importance in my life, namely my travel among primitive and backward communities. This interest began with childhood visits to my father's village birthplace, high in the mountains of Greece, near Corinth. Intrigued at first by the differences in living conditions between the village and home in America, I was gradually made aware of how much people have in common. That observation grew when I spent time among the Hopi in Arizona and, recently, among the Eskimo in Hudson Bay. I look forward to continuing such travels, which provide much insight for my work. I am chiefly interested in finding out how a primitive society such as the early Greek transcends its limitations and becomes an intellectual, urban culture.

A year ago, I met and married a professor who is director of the psychology clinic at the State University of New York at Buffalo. This necessitated my resigning from Brandeis, and although I miss the teaching keenly, I have found a new world of happiness in this marriage. Whereas the first gave me a certain breadth and sharpness of mind, the second makes possible a much greater growth in depth and sensibility, a personal and professional fulfillment that I otherwise might not have obtained. For that reason I have preferred not to continue using my former name even for professional purposes, but to assume that of my husband, even at the risk of mild confusion.

The question perhaps arises at this point which any woman may ask: Did the pursuit of a career, even one aimed at scholarship rather than ego gratification or economic gain, "wreck" my first marriage? In retrospect, no. The failure of the marriage was due to an immaturity and lack of understanding on both sides, and would have happened under any circumstances. Actually, what kept it going for 15 years, in addition to the children, was precisely the intellectual stimulation and interest we had in each other. My first husband would have found me, as a full-time homemaker and dedicated wife, an intolerable bore and would have left much sooner, and my second husband would never have looked at me. Career and marriage can and do mix happily; it is only a combination of certain kinds of people that do not. When they do mix well, then the whole family thrives, as ours does now on all counts. My husband and I are relishing domesticity, enjoying work and independent research more than ever. The children are doing very well and happily.

The only drawback so far has been that I do not have a teaching position. For the second time I am up against a nepotism ruling, this time one which can not easily be bypassed. At the State University the ruling is a carry-over from Depression times, as are all such rulings in universities, initiated to insure one breadwinner, and not more, to each family within a given institution. It was a fair ruling for special conditions. Yet it continues to apply at a time when student population is exploding and there is a constant search at this university and others for additional faculty members. This antediluvian discrimination, either against a woman or wife or both, has been the hardest single, constant factor that I have had to buck in my life. I use the word "buck" advisedly, because often it is like running one's head against a wall that suddenly and arbi-

trarily pops up in professional quarters. As a student trained
in coeducational schools, I was not prepared for the discrimination against women which cropped up the moment I entered
in the professional world. The department in which I studied
for years at Columbia told me outright that they expected I
would settle for marriage rather than a career, and consequently they did nothing whatever to help me obtain a suitable
teaching position. Thereupon I made the second time-consum-
ing, wasteful step in my life; I continued to teach at the secondary school level *after* obtaining my Ph.D. It took years of
publication to prove that in spite of marriage and babies I was
serious about scholarship.

In my first teaching position I found how wretchedly paid
women teachers in girls' private schools are as compared with
men teachers. It became more painful when I saw discrimination extended within the same institution, whereby a woman
who was the sole support of aged and ailing parents received
considerably less than a bachelor for an equivalent position. It
is that kind of observation which quickly converts one to ad-
vocating the Medicare program. For a number of years I
taught 5 days a week, five classes a day, plus extra duties, and
made enough money for lunch, carfare, a baby-sitter, a few
nice clothes *and* state and federal income tax. It was never
more than $2400 a year. I broke about even financially, but it
was worth it because it made possible a little free time in
which to do research and writing.

How many women think it makes sense to do that? Few,
and they are right. Why a man can deduct expenses for a secretary, clerical help, charwoman, for his electric light and
heating bills, and so on, and a working woman cannot deduct
what she pays for domestic help at home, is a prime example of
how women are treated as second-class citizens. If we were to
allow women to deduct from their taxable income the money
spent on such assistance while they are engaged in teaching
and such worthwhile community activities, where they are

badly needed and for which they are best suited, then our whole society would benefit incalculably. Such a deduction would release a large working force of potential teachers, social workers, and others with useful professions who would gladly leave the scrubbing and ironing to someone else for a few hours a day, provided they had something to show for it at the end of the year. It is absurd for a country that can benefit so much from mothers' taking jobs to force them into retirement just as they develop greater understanding of the young.

For myself, even after the jobs of shabby salary were left behind, there was still a certain price which I had to pay for being a woman, again in regard to salary scale. Yet, I must say, gladly and gratefully, that in all other respects the institution at which I taught was as generous and considerate as could be. However, though I taught as many hours, published as much, and received as many foundation grants and honors as men, my salary was always at the bottom for any particular rank. It was presumed that my husband supported me even though the work I accomplished was at least commensurate with the better standards of the university. Otherwise, I would not have received tenure.

On thinking it over, perhaps it was not so much the fact that I was a woman, but that I was married which made for some degree of professional discrimination. Had I been totally dedicated to my career and lost something of my sexual identity, it is possible that I would have been accepted at full status. Early in my professional career, however, I knew I had to remain feminine in dress and manners rather than become the heavy-handed mannish type or even the faded tailored woman. I wear long earrings when I please, and delight in colorful, attractive clothes. It cheers everyone up, and me most of all. A distinctly feminine style of dress, which began partly as compensation for a small stature, has become a necessary and agreeable part of my life. Emphasis on the feminine has actually affected favorably my teaching and research, besides my personal life, obviously. If I could not be a woman first and foremost, I could not be much of anything else. It has been pointed out to me repeatedly that, in my research, I see and analyze cultural problems in a way that no man can and the contribution has value for precisely that reason. Moreover, I don't compete with men in terms of teaching and research— I'm not a man. It is important for a woman to remain one in her work, especially where insight is required, and not to adopt a neutral gender or to pretend that her sex does not count. It does, and it should if each human being is to make his contribution to the cultural betterment of his time. But I am not a militant feminist, nor do I abuse the feminine prerogative; I just wish to be free to be as I am and creative in terms of family and intellectual endeavor.

No human being can have too much education if education is his desire and aptitude permits. Improvement of the mind in every way that can increase human understanding is the obligation of every human being. All of life's beneficent activities contribute to this, such as raising a happy, hard-working family, having warm and worthwhile friends, a deeply pleasurable sex life, travel among illuminating people and places, and making a conscious effort to use one's mind creatively, even if one is not blessed with obvious talents.

I expect to resume teaching for as long as I can, and to retire as late as possible. After that, I shall continue in research and enjoy the companionship of my husband, my grandchildren, friends, books, and Greece.

SUMMARY

We can see from these eight life histories that the tie that binds these planners together is not their goals, but the way in which *planning* has played a crucial role in the patterning of their lives. Their underlying preoccupation with giving a particular shape and structure to their lives and their continuing efforts to realize their respective goals establishes a bond among these otherwise different women.

And they are different. Some are work oriented, some are family oriented and others have sought to combine both work and home. Many who work are satisfied just to have jobs sometimes even part-time jobs. Others are deeply committed to careers.

A common characteristic is that these women realized that whether they wanted a career, or a home, or both, they could fulfill their hopes and desires only if they were willing to pay a price, frequently a high price, to accomplish their primary ends. A goal not backed by a willingness to sacrifice for it is not likely to be realized. The striking fact about these women has been their willingness to pay the tariff. If one could prepare for and pursue a career only by delaying or foregoing marriage, then marriage would have to be delayed or foregone. Similarly, if one wanted a husband and children above all else, she might have to put aside, or at least postpone, her career objectives. The price that a woman is willing to pay to accomplish an end is a key to the importance that she attaches to competing goals.

Despite the fact that these women's present circumstances are largely the product of their planning, the element of luck cannot be completely discounted. Many women with strong desires to reach specific goals are deflected from realizing their aspirations because of the circumstances that they encounter. A would-be careerist may encounter discrimination in employment. A mother who prefers to remain at home may because of financial need have to work. A mother who desires to work may encounter opposition from her husband or may be unable to find a competent housekeeper. A married woman may be bound by the exigencies of her husband's career.

Most women in this group, however, have not been impeded by circumstances. Some encountered discrimination in their careers but were nevertheless able to make satisfactory progress in their work. In general, their husbands are affluent enough and their marriages secure enough to permit those who planned to stay home to do so. The husbands of the working mothers have been encouraging and helpful and satisfactory domestic assistance has been available. Their husbands' jobs have not significantly interfered with their own careers.

Of course, there was more to it than luck. Planning involves successive efforts aimed at exploiting opportunities and overcoming obstacles. These women had the good fortune to confront many opportunities and they had the resources to make the most of them.

The Recasters

The *recasters* are women who make a major change in the patterning of their lives. They are planners who do not carry out their original plans, either because they have lost interest or because they have encountered serious obstacles or attractive new opportunities along the way which they can neither surmount nor ignore.

Some women become recasters because their original values and goals lose their attraction and pull. Suddenly or slowly they find themselves responding to a different set of values and goals. Others become recasters because of an environmental situation. They find that they are unable to realize their original ends. No reasonable amount of effort on their part will dissolve the barriers they encounter and they are unable to find a way around them.

Although these women redesign the patterns of their lives out of desire or necessity, they do so in a manner which retains, rather than destroys, the continuity between the past and the present. When they find that their original solutions for combining the strategic variables in their lives have failed them, they seek to find new and more satisfactory solutions.

"Recasting" refers to the process more than to the elements which comprise the process. In some instances it appears as if entirely new elements were introduced, such as when a woman who originally chooses an occupation in the humanities shifts to medicine. But typically, the shift is less radical, such as when a woman with early interest in the law studies graduate economics only to return to law later on.

The striking point is that many women who change their goals because of new occupational interests have made earlier decisions about a career. But these do not last. A forewarning that this might happen can be deduced from the fact that some women have difficulty in committing themselves to their first career choice. They make their initial decision slowly, usually not in college nor even early in graduate school, but later.

Others make occupational choices that they like; they want to stay with them but this turns out to be impractical. They become recasters because their original plans have foundered on the hard rock of reality. Some women, for instance, discover that their original choice of field is incompatible with the careers of the men whom they marry.

There are others who also knew what they wanted and had every reason to expect that they could realize their plans, but fate treated them harshly. Some looked forward to having families but found themselves childless. Others looked forward to a long married life only to find themselves widowed early.

The key to the necessity to recast for many of these women was found in their marriages. Marriage presented many women with new opportunities, just as it presented others with new pressures and limitations. Those who confronted opportunities in marriage which they had not originally anticipated were often quick to take advantage of them. This meant that they had to give up their early plans and design new ones. Others became recasters because of the unanticipated pressures which they encountered in their marriages.

The impact of marriage was even more pervasive. In general, educated women tend to have small families and within a relatively few years the home no longer is filled with young children. A potent force encouraging women to recast the pattern of their lives and work is the inevitable change that time brings about in homemaking and child rearing. Some women had allowed for the inevitable changes in their original planning. But many others did not. For them, the only way out was to recast their lives.

A SHIFT OF INTEREST

Time itself leads to changes in an individual's interests and goals. Exposures and experiences are never neutral. They affect the individual in one way or another. Some tend to have a constructive impact, and these often lead to a reordering of an individual's desires.

Since most young people must decide on their future occupations without having had any work experience or any relevant work experience, it is surprising that so many remain satisfied with the choices they made in school. It is less surprising that some young adults, when they finally begin to work after finishing their education, find a wide and disturbing discrepancy between their expectations about work and the reality which they confront. Some of them, perhaps most, are able to make adjustments in their work or in other sectors of their lives, and to stay with their original choices. But others are too dissatisfied to compromise. They have no option but to reopen the whole question of their careers and seek other choices that will better meet their needs and desires. A change in interest is one antecedent to the recasting of one's life.

A shift of interest may appear relatively early or fairly late in life. Some women discover in graduate school that their fields of choice are incompatible with their interests or abilities. Others find, somewhat later after work experience, that their chosen fields do not meet their expectations. Still others may have no particularly negative reaction to their fields but find, after a hiatus for child rearing, that newly developed concerns have superseded their earlier interests.

Sometimes a shift of interest may be quite radical and may require long years of additional training. In other instances, the shift may be minor and the recaster is able to build upon her old skills in pursuing her new occupation.

For some women, the identification and pursuit of new interests is relatively easy. They may have both sufficient inner resources and sufficient personal and financial support from their husbands to prepare for their new undertakings. Other women, however, take a great deal of time convincing themselves that their first choices were mistakes and in seeking substitute goals. They may sample several possibilities before finding suitable niches for themselves, and sometimes, in the course of psychotherapy, they become able to develop new interests and to respond to new opportunities.

Natalie Goodman

My parents were respectable, if not outstanding, members of a middle-class community. They could afford to send me to college and were willing to do so. Like most others in our milieu they had little occupational information, and consequently I was left to my own devices in choosing courses and majors. Both my parents were American born and had graduated from high school. My father was a builder who was unemployed or marginally employed during the Depression in the early thirties.

I am the older of two children. My brother, 7 years my junior, is now a graduate student in biochemistry. I was born in Cincinnati and was brought up in Los Angeles. I entered Simmons College in 1938 when I was 17 and transferred to Northwestern in my sophomore year, where I was an honors

student in political theory. My parents wanted me to be "educated" as a mark of social status and in order to achieve upward mobility through marriage. I did marry in 1942, the year
I graduated from college, and in marrying early and accept-
ably I undoubtedly was reflecting their attitude. By working I
reflect my own.

My husband is a physician. During the first year of our marriage, I attended secretarial school. Then I accompanied him to
Texas, where he served in the Army, and I worked as a secretary at the same post. World War II restricted the develop-
mental opportunities open to both of us. The immediate post-
war years were difficult for my husband, particularly, in finding opportunity for advanced training. The war had the effect
of postponing full maturity for both of us. We went to New
York in 1944 and I entered the Columbia Graduate School of
Business to study labor relations.

My original goal in college had been to work in Latin American affairs, but I changed my mind before graduation. I decided to prepare for a field of work since my A.B. was not oc-
cupationally oriented. I had always been interested in the role
of trade unions and thought I would like to work in labor research. During the second year of my studies I had a part-time
job in a trade union research department preparing materials
for collective bargaining. This gave me access to materials for
my master's thesis.

The following year, after I received my M.S., we moved to
Philadelphia where I worked part-time for 4 months on a public health project at the University of Pennsylvania. I gave
birth to my first child that year, and I stayed home and did not
work (except as a volunteer) for 10 years from the birth of
our first child until the second one was 7.

My volunteer activities have included work in politics for
the last 5 years and as a youth group leader for 2 years. My
main reason for volunteer participation has been a belief in the

efficacy of citizen participation as a way of influencing events. It is gratifying to work with others to achieve political or social results. But this type of activity needs a "self-starter" since there are no regular responsibilities. Furthermore, both the competition for status and the amateur status itself are frustrating.

We moved to Boston where I took Russian courses in the early fifties as an unmatriculated student at Harvard. Languages had always been a strong secondary interest but I found that available work opportunities were not sufficiently attractive or challenging at my low level of proficiency. I was never up to literary work.

In 1956 I entered the Boston University School of Education to prepare for a Ph.D. in human relations. I thought of this as a field which would combine my interests and previous training in youth development and manpower problems. At Columbia I had entered a new field which I built on, to some extent, at BU. While there have been discontinuities, the earlier training did influence my subsequent interests in manpower and education. I considered this second period of graduate study as not only occupational preparation but as a means of returning to the labor market after many years absence. I spent 2 years in full-time study and engaged in some small fact-gathering projects. After completing my course requirements, I worked on the State Report for the President's Committee for the Employment of Youth and, at the end of this project, I worked as a research associate for two foundations engaged in research on education and youth employment.

Since 1961, when I received my Ph.D., I have held an executive position with the Boston branch of a federal agency, where I deal with the analysis and review of apprenticeship programs. This was the natural agency for the kind of work I wanted to do. I find my work interesting and my preparation adequate, especially as I have been able to draw on the variety in my background. I like being involved in a small way in a major issue of the day and I enjoy the stimulation of the job and of my colleagues. I dislike the pressure of deadlines, my tendency to overwork, and a preoccupation with next steps. And I also dislike the occasional traveling required in my work. Yet, I probably would not change my field, although, if an academic position were available, I might change the milieu.

Until 1958, most of my jobs represented simply an opportunity to do something fairly interesting. There was no attempt at a career line. The major change from labor relations to my present work was due partly to lack of opportunity and inadequate training and partly to the need to start over after a long period of absence from the labor market.

The enthusiasm of my husband was important to the pursuit of my studies and he has been unusually supportive in furthering my career. The children created a hiatus, especially in motivation, but were not a hindrance to my doing graduate study. Since I undertook all my graduate education after marriage, I was quite aware of the difficulties of combining a career with adequate child rearing. I probably could not work without household assistance. I have been extremely fortunate in having had the same exceedingly competent housekeeper for 7 years. At present, the children's needs restrict certain of my leisure and volunteer activities but not my work.

I may be at home less than other women, but I feel that the time I do spend at home is more pleasant and useful for the rest of the family than it was when I was not working. The children do more for themselves. I get great satisfaction from helping them mature and from the creation of positive family feeling. I also enjoy cooking and entertaining. When I have time I play some tennis and go sailing, but among my leisure activities, reading is most important, as it fulfills some need for escape, and physical release is not so important at my present fatigue level. I still have some occasional unpleasant homemaking chores to perform such as shopping, running errands, supervising the housekeeping, doing the family accounts, cleaning, and sewing.

We have lived in several cities as my husband's career demanded. We live in the city, rather than in a suburb, mostly because of my activities. I think I appreciate my husband's work problems better because my own experiences are similar. There is a value in knowing what the real world is like. In addition, the income I make has made it possible for him to concentrate on doing what he likes rather than being burdened by the need to provide additional income. Our combined income is over $30,000 a year. I never expected to live as affluently as I do. I don't anticipate any major changes in our activities, except that when the children grow up, we may be free to travel more.

I do not want to make general prescriptions, but I do feel that women should be encouraged in their efforts to acquire a higher education and to work. These opportunities have been of enormous importance to me. My education has determined my work, which is a major preoccupation and has also contributed to our middle-class, somewhat intellectual life-style. The great advantage of being a woman is the possibility of receiving financial support for education and the greater freedom in choice of job and other things when the family does not depend on this income. I have had both of these advantages. On the other hand, I lack geographical mobility, I am paid less than men with comparable ability, and there are problems in supervising men at work.

I have become accustomed to a full-time job with quite heavy responsibilities. It would be easier if many jobs could be redefined to permit part-time work. Since this is possible in only a few fields at present, I feel it worthwhile to carry on as I do at present. My case is probably unusual. I have had every kind of help, and I am doing work I like. I can imagine that if there had been more difficulties, the game might not have seemed worth the candle.

Daphne Upton

In 1940, at the age of 13, I was evacuated to this country from London, where I was born. I resided with a professor of history at Wellesley College and still feel very close to him, his wife, and his family. My foster father, who spent his life educating women, was proud of women who achieved and I grew up hearing about these women. They seemed to be able to surmount great odds, to be particularly creative and to have great energy. How did they do it? And what about their families? I do not have so much dedication myself, but part of me feels I should, too!

My own father was a traveling salesman with a grade school education. My mother, who had a similar educational background, worked in an office before she married and later when I was in high school worked as a librarian. She has recently become a lay preacher after 3 years of study. Before that she did volunteer work in a hospital two afternoons a week. She considered her interests outside the home and the ability to support herself at an interesting job very important. My parents were always concerned about their own lack of education and wanted my older brother and me to be educated. My brother is now a professor of pharmacology.

I attended high school in Wellesley and entered Wellesley College in 1944, where I majored in economics. By graduation, I had decided to go to graduate school and possibly to teach. I was granted scholarship aid from Columbia, and after receiving my B.A., I enrolled in the graduate department of economics. I was on a student visa and this was a means of staying in

this country. I was very confused about my future and did not
know if I wanted to live in England or America. I had no real
career goals, though I was interested in marriage as a long-
range goal. Graduate study would give me more time to make
up my mind. School was what I knew and I had to do something. Since economics had been my undergraduate interest, it
was my choice for graduate work. I discovered subsequently
that my interest in undergraduate economics was really an interest in people and how they lived rather than an interest in
the market place, and graduate economics was not my "cup of
tea." I could see little point and felt no interest in the minutiae
of theoretical discussion. Higher economics also became more
mathematical, and this again was not my interest.

After a year of study, I took a summer job as a bank clerk
and then returned to England for a few months. I decided to
become an American citizen, returned here, and took a research job with the Census Bureau. I thought I might be interested in research but found it to be unrewarding, tedious, and
uncreative. Although I received my M.A. in economics in
1950, I decided to test a growing interest in social work and
became a part-time group worker for a project sponsored by a
social welfare council in Cleveland. I received $40 a week plus
my living. It was little more than an experience with group living but it gave me time to begin studying social work part-
time at Western Reserve in order to learn more about the
field.

After a year of study, I gave up the thought of further
graduate work when I became involved in psychotherapy,
which I thought was going to be short-term. I could not afford
school and therapy and did not have the emotional energy for
both. As it turned out, I was in therapy for 6 years, 2 or 3
times a week. This has been a major influence on my life.

When the group work project ended, I could not get into
public welfare work since I was not yet a citizen, so I became

an underwriting assistant for an insurance company. After 2 years, I left because business, like economics and research, was just not satisfying to me and did not call forth any creative resources I might have. Since I had become a citizen in 1954, I was hired by the Ohio State Welfare Department as a public assistance caseworker. I wanted to work with people and to see if I was suited for social work. I found that I do like working with people not only as clients but as co-workers. It is just plain good to be involved. I like "using my head," too. Also, sex discrimination does not seem to be such a problem in social work as in other fields. I was promoted to supervisor in the same division after four years.

I was married in 1961, at the age of 34, to a psychiatric social worker who had a job with the state department of mental health. Our place of residence has been influenced by our respective jobs. When we were married, we settled midway between them. I left the welfare department the following year when I was about to have a baby, and stayed home for a while. After full-time employment for years, housework left me dazed after a while. I enjoy seeing my baby grow and taking care of him and my husband. I like to cook also. But housekeeping is physically taxing. I don't get much chance to sit and do nothing and that would be nice! Sometimes the constant responsibility gets me.

When my son was 7 months old, I became a part-time worker for a community service agency where I judge casework profiles and other research. I was interested in the program and I needed the money because my husband was in graduate school.

I now spend 10 to 15 hours weekly on the job and the rest at home. My housekeeping chores take precedence, but I feel like a juggler. I don't have much time to myself for such things as reading, and since my work is part-time, some of it is strictly clerical, although I have responsibility. My husband was in

favor of my returning to work, but now that he is again working full-time, he is ambivalent. He feels it is too tiring for me
and that if we should need more money, he should get a second job. Our combined annual income is between $16,000 and
$17,000. Since my pay has been adequate, I have been able to
afford help and could not have worked without it. Help has
been readily available.

It has meant a great deal to me to work during the last year.
Obviously, it was a minimal amount but it still got me out of
the house and helped me realize my own identity apart from
my family. When I went back to work it was even an experience to drive into Cleveland from the suburb where we live—a
distance of 12 miles. But there have been some dreadful mo-
ments—what do you do if the weather is bad and the baby sitter has trouble getting to you—or what happens if your child
is sick—or if the job turns out to be too much for what you
can give it and you are committed to finishing it? However, I
do think that the exposure my son has had to other people because I have worked has been good for him. I don't believe
that spending one or two days a week with another person he
likes is going to traumatize him. On the contrary, it gives him
a new experience. However, he still puts up a fuss when I leave
and this is a little hard to take even though he stops when he
finds it doesn't pay dividends.

Obviously, if I don't work it will be because I am needed at
home. I really don't like leaving my child, and have limited my
work time and kept change of sitters to the minimum. Several
times recently, I have taken my son with me to work for brief
periods in order not to have to get a new sitter. I expect to
have another baby in about 8 months so that will scratch any
plans I might have for further part-time work, at least for the
next few years. It is just too hard to combine activities. As a
recent article indicated, many women work when they have

only one child; it is the second child that ends a career unless one has a highly developed skill or has a profession such as medicine.

What will I do to keep up and maintain an interest in my field? My husband helps tremendously since he is in the same field; our common interest helps us and makes our home life livelier. I'll continue to read his professional magazines and he'll prod every now and then about my getting out and doing something in an area of my concern. So far, I have not proved to myself that I can be individually creative, i.e., work on my own—so I don't know what the next step is. I may decide, eventually, to change to a field that would fit more into family life, school vacations, and so on, for I know I will wish to be home when the children are. This may turn out to be school work, but whether I stay in my present field or switch to education, I will want further schooling. I still wish I had a master's degree in social work because there are so many more part-time jobs for people who have that degree.

I've done a little volunteer work with my local alumnae club and as a hospital volunteer. I was interested in the work and I enjoyed being with people, but I don't like the lack of responsibility in volunteer activity. When I have time, I read for relaxation and stimulation, and I redo furniture which allows for some creativity.

It seems to me that the more specifically trained a woman is, the better chance she has of continuing to take care of her family and to have a part-time career. I did not think that far ahead when I was in graduate school. Now I know it takes a great deal of energy to work when one has babies, and it isn't always possible. From my own point of view, the task of combining home and career does not lend itself to a permanent solution, just to temporary resolutions. When I told my foster mother, who herself wanted to be an artist, about the questionnaire supplied for this survey, she said that the problem could be stated by a simple four-letter word: "time." I would also add "energy."

The questionnaire asked, in what way has my formal education contributed to my way of life. What a question! How do you separate what you know from who you are? I was depressed during my school years, and the intervening years have been rugged as I worked through to some sort of balance. Offhand, these years have been more exciting, challenging, and rewarding than I could have visualized when I was at school.

FAMILY INFLUENCE

When a woman marries, the terms of her life change, frequently drastically. But the nature of the changes is difficult to foretell. Therefore, many women find that marriage has produced conditions that have no place in their early plans, and they often recast their goals in light of these new circumstances.

Sometimes a marriage provides supportive circumstances, such as a husband who encourages a woman to pursue a new career. Some families' finances may be such that a woman who had anticipated leaving her job to raise her children finds that she can afford to hire domestic help and to continue working. And sometimes a woman with initially strong career goals finds that she prefers to remain at home with her children and is able to do so.

On the other hand, marriage may present obstacles to the fulfillment of early goals and lead to recasting of these plans. A woman may find her career goals thwarted by her husband's inability to cover the expenses of her working outside the home. Or her husband may prefer that she give up her work in order to take care of her home. Another woman may discover that if the marriage is to flourish she must not compete in the work area with her husband. Another influential antecedent to the process of recasting is divorce or widowhood, either of which may compel a woman to give up her preference for homemaking in favor of work.

For some single women, there is what might be called a negative family influence. These are women who expected to marry and raise families and did not. In this unanticipated position they reappraise their goals and are able to commit themselves to their work without too much regret. They have been forced to recast their plans but they derive considerable satisfaction from their new goals.

Thus, we see that for some women family influences present opportunities far beyond their early anticipation. Others are impelled to lead more restricted lives than they had anticipated. Nevertheless, none of these women is so disquieted by the change in her plans that she is unable to function adequately in her new role.

Frances Hazen

My parents felt a woman's place was in the *home* and thought a woman should definitely *not* be gainfully employed. They did, however, feel a woman should be educated and were able to and did provide me with a college education. Both of them were born in Poland and emigrated to the United States as adults. My father, a rabbi, was a graduate of a rabbinical seminary. My mother had no formal education and no work experience but she was literate. I was born in San Francisco in 1923 and lived there until I entered Stanford Uni-

versity when I was 16. I have two older sisters, one a housewife. The other is a business woman, and our parents' attitudes
with respect to women working did not deter either of us.

At college I majored in political science and planned to go
on to law school. However, my parents objected to a law career for a woman and so I applied to Columbia for a scholarship for graduate work. I wished to leave home and was at-
tracted by New York. I was awarded a sizable grant and enrolled in the Department of Public Law and Government in
1944, since a continuation of my undergraduate major seemed
most sensible. I considered social work but was deterred by
the time and money involved in such a change.

I received my master's degree in 1945 and worked as a research associate at Stanford for 6 months to see if I would like
the academic world. My primary objection to completing the
Ph.D. was that I felt it would be a serious disadvantage in reference to marriage; I felt it would hinder my getting married.
However, when I did marry in 1946, my husband, a rabbi
with an M.A. and a rabbinical degree, urged me to complete
the doctorate and I returned to Columbia and made some mild
attempts to do so. But I found graduate school government
courses a repetition of undergraduate ones and my work experience at Stanford convinced me that an academic life was not
for me. Academic political science impressed me as much talk,
and the obvious made complicated. It had very little permanent attraction.

From 1947 until 1953 I stayed home, gave birth to two children, and engaged in some volunteer work largely concerned
with various women's groups, such as the League of Women
Voters, religious organizations, political clubs, and human relations agencies. I enjoy meeting people and doing what I can
for those things and causes in which I believe. It is good to aid
the cause to which I subscribe and to help to see it through to
fruition, despite the petty details involved in committee meet-

ings. As a wife and mother, my deepest gratifications are in the companionship of my husband and the great pleasure and responsibility of rearing children and participating in their development and growth.

I resisted any prospects of working during the early years of my marriage when my children were young. But the years passed, and my husband insisted that I go to law school and develop a career for myself, rather than spend my entire life in domestic chores. Therefore, in 1953, I entered Gonzaga University Law School in Spokane, Washington where we were living. Law was what I had always wanted, and although I felt guilty about leaving my children while attending law school, as they grow older, I am delighted that I made the decision. Having my husband's full and complete cooperation was the most important factor in my return to school.

After receiving my LL.B. in 1956, I established my own private law practice in Spokane. I am still at it and I love it. I spend about 40 hours a week working at my practice and about 4 to 5 hours in volunteer work which, in addition to some of my earlier interests, now includes professional associations and membership and occasional leadership of a study group. I continue my education through bar courses to keep abreast of the constant changes in the law and legal procedures.

Self-employment determines everything I do. I enjoy working with people, solving their problems, furthering the great system of law and jurisprudence under which we live—and making money ($9,000 to $10,000 a year). The only things I don't like are the petty complications, the burdensome paper work and the red tape still required in many legal procedures. The only change that could possibly occur in my career would be a judicial appointment or a decision to run for political office. Self-employment enables me to arrange for time with my children when necessary or desirable. Household help is always a problem but we manage. Taxes have no effect on my decisions whatsoever. My husband's income is between $15,000 and $20,000 a year.

Women in the practice of law have a disadvantage in the attitudes both of male attorneys who consider them interlopers and of clients who evidence some lack of confidence in a female, particularly in areas of business and corporate law. However, we can always win confidence and respect by proving our ability and doing a better job without any "chips on the shoulder." Being a woman is in itself sufficient compensation for any losses.

I think it is wonderful for a woman to have an education and a career. It provides tremendously important stimulation and satisfaction for those who are interested. It makes her a happier, more sound human and a better wife and mother. However, I do not think that all women need this type of thing and there are some who can be happy by devoting their complete lives to their homes and families. Even for these, an *education* is essential in that they can lead full lives and be better, more interesting and more interest*ed* people.

I do feel that every person should have interests in life, whether that person be male or female. Some women can find satisfaction by being homemakers and clubwomen. Others need more. Many who are now "homemakers" apparently would be far happier if they had some other outside interests and for this reason are resentful and jealous of those women who do. On the other hand, a woman in a career encounters some resentments from men who feel she is competing and insulting their manly prerogatives. Only an insecure male, however, suffers from such great fears of being displaced. To those who are mature, both male and female, it is possible for a woman to have a career, combine it with an entirely satisfactory marriage and home life, and be a better person and mother as a result.

While I personally enjoy my work and find that it is an asset rather than a burden, I am not a "great emancipator" and I do not want to be considered the *equal* of a man in all respects. In other words, I am a woman first and foremost; I work outside the home because it makes me a more complete person and I am fortunate in being able to arrange my time accordingly. I do not wish, however, to abdicate my feminine role, nor to assume the full responsibility of breadwinner our society casts upon the male. I am therefore perfectly willing to be a "woman" in a career and perhaps accept a little less so-called "success" in return for the vast advantages of being "protected" in the home and being seated first at dinner. At the same time, as far as work is concerned, I expect no special advantage because of my sex, and am willing to pay the price of some slight disadvantage which is vastly repaid because I can adopt the feminine role at home and in company.

I think a woman who really wants and expects *full equality* in employment is headed for emotional problems, because that might mean full equality between male and female in all areas of life; it might damage the woman's psyche if she were to achieve the exact opposite of what she really wants.

Mary McLachlan

My father's death in 1923, when I was 12, made it necessary for me to take scholarship possibilities seriously if I wished to attend college. Most of my way through college was paid by scholarships (supplemented by summer work), but I always had my mother's practical and moral support.

My father had been a Canadian farmer with a grade school education. My mother attended normal school and taught until I was born. When she was widowed, she moved to town and educated my brother and me on a small fixed income. She had a chance to teach at one point, but this meant relocating and she preferred not to interrupt my brother's education. He is now a clergyman. My parents both had confidence in my ability as a good student and as a good worker. My brother and I were expected to be serious members of society.

I was born in an Ontario farming community and was graduated from high school in Galt in 1927. I attended the University of Toronto, where I majored in French and Spanish with the intention of teaching in college. As a woman, I was urged to study modern languages rather than mathematics which I would have preferred at the time. I do not now regret it, since, if I had studied mathematics, I probably would not have had an opportunity to study abroad or travel. On the other hand, I sometimes wish I had studied biology, but a career in this field, other than teaching, would still have been difficult.

After receiving my B.A., I spent 2 years studying contemporary French literature at the Sorbonne under a Bourse D'Etudes from the French Government. Upon my return, I needed to work and was hired as a French and Spanish teacher at a boarding school for girls. I left after a year to attend the Ontario College of Education in order to qualify for work in a public high school. The following year I took a job as senior French teacher at a Canadian school in Kobe, since jobs were scarce at home during Depression years.

My 3-year contract expired in 1938 and I went on a round-the-world trip which ended when I married in Hong Kong at the end of that year. In June, 1939, I went to live in England with my husband, who was a civil servant in the admiralty. He had a higher school certificate, which is equivalent to university matriculation, and he had high intellectual ability, but his further education was precluded by the death of his father. For the next two years, I stayed home, first in London, then in Bath, until I was conscripted during the war and taught French and Spanish at a Bath boys' school. I stopped teaching at the end of the war and, when my husband died of cancer in 1946, I returned to Canada, since I then had to earn my living and my prospects for employment seemed better there.

My former French professor at the University of Toronto, who also offered me half-time employment there, recommended me to the University of Manitoba, where I was employed as a full-time instructor in French. If I had accepted the lectureship at Toronto, I might have pursued my studies and have become a French professor. I don't know why I didn't. I said I wanted full-time employment, but I do not think that was the whole reason. Sometimes I have regrets, for in many ways I would have preferred living in a college atmosphere rather than in Ottawa, where I now live, and I would have had more time for travel and friendships. As a civil servant, my present position, I have only a limited vacation. After a year of teaching at the University of Manitoba, I decided to try to qualify for work with the United Nations. I decided not to take an M.A. in French because I was tired of teaching the French language, and I saw little future for me in university teaching. I changed to international affairs because I believed that my training and experience of life in different countries and my world travel had made me a citizen of the world. I entered the Columbia School of International Affairs in 1947, where I was able to use part of a small inheritance to pay expenses. During the following summer I interned at Lake Success, which was a valuable experience, especially the living with students from all over the world.

Since 1949, when I received my Master of International Affairs, I have been working as a researcher and section head for a government office in Ottawa. After spending 2 years at Columbia, I was told by a brash young man who interviewed me for a position at the United Nations that I had four qualifications for the job—English, French, Spanish and charm! I didn't pursue the application. I have always found that it was

more difficult to receive full consideration for employment because of my sex and, in my work, women are not groomed for
promotion. A career is perhaps easier for a woman who wants
to be a specialist rather than a generalist, as I did when I studied at Columbia. And still do. There seems to be less "politics"
involved.

The aspects of my work which I like most are its financial
rewards, the prospect of a pension, and the subject matter of
my research in international affairs. I dislike the "kink" given
to my work by "intelligence," and the security aspects of
being an intelligence analyst. However, only the deterioration
of my health or disappearance of the office would cause me to
change my field again. I have thought of returning to teaching,
but have been deterred by the recollection of the physical and
nervous strain and also by my age, 53, and the loss of my pension. Such a change is still not impossible, however. I will be
able to retire on a pension in 6 years, but I could continue to
work if I wish.

My experiences are disappointing compared to the expectations of my early years. Of course, I graduated during the Depression, there were no openings at the university, and during
the war years in England I could not really work at a career
because of my marriage. I began my second career rather late
in life and arthritis (even when not acute) inhibits some activities.

When I was a homemaker exclusively, I liked the flexible
timetable, time for gardening, hobbies, voluntary activities,
and reading—and the companionship with my husband. Now I
find that household care is the most limiting factor in shaping
my pursuits. My car is the most liberating. In our servantless
world, a woman, single or not, cannot escape household chores
and there is no income tax rebate for a housekeeper, even if
one could be found.

In England, I was interested in political, professional and

adult education activities, and also in an organization to obtain womens' rights. This was the only time in my life that I had time for such activities. When I have free time now, besides driving in the country, I enjoy walking, botanizing and bird watching, reading, and swimming. The outdoor activities are a welcome contrast to a sedentary and intellectually demanding office working life. I also travel during vacations and attend plays and concerts. This year, I have been brushing up on my French. A trip to Mexico last spring meant an opportunity to brush up on a little Spanish as well as to enjoy the sun.

I have reached the stage where I must either take my work less seriously (i.e., not work so hard at the office, or go all out for a short spell only when absolutely necessary), or else have a housekeeper. Since the latter is well-nigh impossible, I have to fall in with the former. My biggest personal problem is to find energy to devote to hobbies (energy even more than time) and to entertain a few personal friends, in ones or twos. The dinner "gap" affects single women of my age. Our social life is restricted by the custom of going in pairs as into Noah's Ark when going to a dinner party, even an informal one.

The twentieth century made possible my education, being able to earn a good livelihood, and having a car, household gadgets, hi-fi, radio, and television, but also condemned me and other single working women to a life of loneliness, such as no family woman, no "religieuse," and no man in our society, married or unmarried, can even guess at. I call working women like me "lay sisters." It's like being a guinea pig, but in the interest of what? Progress? It may be individual progress but at a price. I do not see any social progress, since socially, in the usual sense, career women are ignored (a more accurate term than "not accepted"). There is no slot for them. We are the "forgotten women." The term "bachelor girl" is ambiguous; one never hears "bachelor woman."

I suppose one should be glad that society (in the larger

sense) is making use of one's mental resources and training. But it is done reluctantly and often with bad grace. I do not have the energy (or the time) to play a role in the community, as I did in England. It is not enough just to be part of the national economy. One should also "belong" to society. Only women with "positions," not with jobs, belong to society, however insecurely.

I think married women should work if they wish to and have training. *But* there should be domestic help. With children, the problem of help is even more acute. Too many hours moonlighting make Jill either a dull or too casual worker. A shorter work week (which they say is coming) would benefit career women. I think that I, myself, have always worked too hard. Yet, on looking back, I would urge my nieces, 16 years and 13 years, to get higher education. They are not in danger of working as hard as I did.

It is just possible that by the time I am 60, ready to retire on pension, I shall be mellow. My poor to indifferent health during the past year may have made me lose heart. If I reach retirement at my job! If I do, I'll write my memoirs as a "lay sister"; if not, I suppose I can become a beachcomber.

I think it is a mistake to be a single (i.e., not married) career woman unless one has a very strong sense of vocation. It means very hard work and life gets more grim as one grows older. One has a livelihood and obligations but neither male nor female rewards.

EMPLOYMENT BARRIERS

We know that many boys receive too little occupational guidance to enable them to make the most of their potentialities and education. Girls receive even less. It is not surprising therefore that many young women complete a long education only to find that there are no ready jobs in their fields or only jobs that pay marginal salaries.

An additional occupational problem for women is that most of them have limited mobility. Some must go where their husbands go. Others choose to remain where their parents are. They cannot match their education and training with all the jobs that are available; they often must concentrate on the few in a particular locale.

The passage of the Civil Rights Act of 1965 finally provided for the elimination of all discrimination based on sex, as well as race. But, since women have long suffered from severe discrimination in hiring, training, promotion, and pay, it is unlikely that the law will be able to eliminate all of these discriminatory practices in the near future. Thus, women may find that desirable job opportunities are limited because men continue to be favored.

Another hurdle that many women face in finding employment derives from the policies that many institutions have established to avoid nepotism. Many universities, government agencies, and other employers will not hire two members of the same family, surely not in the same department. Since young women frequently marry professional colleagues, many of them find that if they want to work, they must recast their career objectives.

Eve Gottlieb

My parents, who had limited schooling themselves, encouraged my younger sister and me to take advantage of our opportunities for education in order to have the interesting lives which had been denied to them. My father was a Czech-born dress manufacturer whose business failed during the Depression. My mother, who was born in the United States, worked in a factory prior to her marriage and returned to work as a sales clerk when I was in college, at first because of financial need, and later, to keep busy.

I was born in New York in 1922. My family's straitened finances made it necessary for me to pay my own way from an early age, but this did not deter me from any of my decisions or goals. I attended Hunter College from 1939 to 1943 and majored in biology. I hoped to complete the course of study and work in a laboratory job related to medical sciences. I also expected, or hoped, that I would get married and raise a family. While in college I worked for the National Youth Administration, and as a baby-sitter, a tutor, and factory worker. These were important to the development of my self-reliance and independence.

After graduation I worked as a laboratory chemist for a home products manufacturer in New Jersey but left after 8 months because I wanted to live in a city where I could take courses. Therefore, I returned to New York, where I was able to attend evening classes in biology. After 3 months of looking for a job, I became panicky and took a job in a hospital as a lab technician. It sounded much better than it turned out to be; I finally left the following year, because the work was dull and uninteresting and the supervisor was extremely inconsiderate.

At the end of 1944, I obtained employment with the local department of health as a junior bacteriologist. I was interested in the field and the job seemed better than the one I had had before. A year later, a professor at the Columbia School of Public Health offered me what seemed a better opportunity as a lab technician assisting in research. After 8 months, I started taking courses at the school towards an M.S. degree in parasitology, and worked fewer hours. I paid full tuition to Columbia and was given a salary deduction for time spent in class. I took 40 credits over a period of 2 academic years. I realized that if I wished to advance in laboratory work, in which I had a continuing interest, graduate work was necessary. My main interest was in microbiology but the bacteriology department did not take candidates for masters degrees. Since I was not sure I wanted to work for a Ph.D., and I was already working in parasitology, I decided to pursue that course of study in the School of Public Health.

After receiving my M.S. in 1948, I went to Sweden, where I sought a university job primarily as a means of supporting myself while engaging in the exciting adventure of traveling and living in a foreign country. I became a graduate assistant in the bacteriology department of a scientific institute in Stockholm and, at the same time, took courses toward a doctoral degree. I did not complete my thesis requirement because during my two years in Sweden, I took stock of my own capabilities, ambitions, and interests, and of how I could apply these best to get—and give—the most in life. I decided that the future I wanted for myself did not exist in the sciences. I was not a creative thinker who could direct whole projects—I was a top-rate first assistant.

I returned to the United States in 1951 and worked for the next two years in part-time and temporary assignments in laboratories under special grants in order to earn a living while seeking a permanent job. In 1953, after 4 years of specialized (post B.A.) experience, 2 or 3 years of related experience, plus my M.S. degree, the Columbia University department which had granted me my master's degree offered me a salary of $2,500 with no opportunity for improvement. I did consider the federal civil service, which was the best possibility if I decided to remain within my specialization, but I decided to change, since I had not found what I had earlier anticipated—a scientific job at an intermediate level between the technicians and the top-level planners and directors, a level at which a significant and helpful contribution could be made by a research assistant who was competent, interested, conscientious, but not necessarily creative. I had found instead that no matter how much experience you had, you were still called a technician and were paid cleaning woman's wages. Often you might be doing the work of a research assistant, but you were not given the title or respect for your capabilities.

In 1953 I found a position in scientific editorial work for a publishing house. This permitted me to combine an interest in writing with my training in the sciences. I have continued in this field and presently serve largely in an administrative and supervisory capacity. I started at an annual salary of $3,000 and now make about three times as much. I find my work challenging, interesting, and stimulating. The office atmosphere is pleasant and I am buoyed by the knowledge that I do my job well, even if it is not world-shaking in importance. Of course, the best and most satisfying job has its tedious or frustrating moments, but there is no one thing I can single out as particularly unsatisfactory, unless it be the overall factor of not making any particular contribution to the progress of the world—but how many people really do? Actually I can think of no condition under which I would change my present field, since even if I were to marry and have greater family obligations I could continue in this work with fewer hours per week.

As it is, I keep house for myself only, and am gratified to have a comfortable, tasteful, relaxing place in which I can be myself. My only regret is that I do not have a mate to share this with. I spend many hours as a director and committee member for the interracial housing cooperative in which I live. I was a settlement house volunteer from 1958 to 1960 and have been a member and officer of my local college alumni organization. I participate in those activities which I find of interest. I found my welfare work satisfying because I felt we were doing something positive. My present hours at the co-op are important because this is my home and I believe in the principle of this type of housing and living. Unfortunately, people in groups frequently waste time—which I cannot afford. There's really not enough time for all the things I would like to do, but, in addition to my volunteer activities, I also try to find time for photography, both taking pictures and the processing, tropical fish, reading, traveling, concert and theatre going, entertaining and visiting my family and friends, and walking in the park. Which of these I indulge in depends on my frame of mind at any moment.

In conclusion, I wish to say that each woman must decide for herself whether she wants to study, what she wants to study, if she can handle both family obligations and job, and other decisions of this nature. There is no one answer. I read a lot and hear a lot about womanpower or talent being lost because women with college degrees stay at home to raise families. But I am not impressed. I have known far too many women whose college degrees did not signify much at all in the way of talent or potential contribution.

Noreen Nadler

I was born in New York in 1926 and have lived there all my life. My father was born in Boston and my mother, in Toronto. Neither of them went beyond grade school. My father is employed as a furniture maker and my mother worked only before her marriage. My parents believed in education, work, and marriage for me and I never thought of anything else.

I attended Queens College, where I majored in Latin and minored in Greek. I knew when I entered college that I wanted to teach these languages in college, and I never swerved from that goal throughout my education. I was graduated in 1946 and received a scholarship for graduate study in the Greek and Latin department at Columbia. My love of

learning and of my major subjects, plus the ambition to become a college teacher, influenced my decision to pursue further schooling. The scholarship, and later awards from Columbia, for which I have always been grateful, made the decision possible. I chose the humanities because they presented
the widest scope and seemed to deal with those ideas and
values that were closest to the understanding of life.

I studied at Columbia from 1946 through 1949, receiving my
M.A. in 1947. During my studies I did some small amount of
substitute teaching at Hunter College which led directly to
three years of full-time employment in the classics department
there, from 1949 to 1952. However, I was ineligible for reap-
pointment beyond three years, since I lacked the Ph.D. I had
completed my residence requirements and passed my examinations in classics, but never finished my dissertation.

I spent the next 5 months seeking employment, but there
were no opportunities to continue teaching in New York and I
have been confined to this area because of the need to remain
with my mother, who has not been well. Personnel offices
could see no relationship between my background in classics
and the specialized work they offered. My teaching experience
was never considered favorably in any job interview. From the
point of view of personnel management, no matter what the
job, only the specialist is qualified to fill it. Until a very recent
marked change in the attitude of the business world to scholarship, liberal training was held in small regard, and a background in ancient classics still counts for nothing.

I finally took a job as an invoice clerk with a large chemical
firm in New York, at a starting salary of $42 a week. This was
the only position offered to me after many months of searching. I am still working for the same organization but I have
had periodic promotions and am now employed in electronic
data processing after having been given the opportunity to

take courses in programming and systems analysis. I earn about $130 a week.

I spend 40 hours a week at my job and 10 hours studying ancient languages, reading archaeology and philosophy, and attempting to complete my doctoral thesis. The degree of M.A. made it possible to begin my teaching career. The lack of the doctorate made it impossible to continue it. I also spend about one hour a week administering a scholarship awards program on behalf of an honorary academic society. At work, I have congenial colleagues and a pleasant environment and I am grateful for the opportunity to become acquainted with the huge and complicated structure of a modern accounting operation, including recent developments in electronics. Furthermore, I take pride in my association with a company that has national and international importance and a good reputation. But until recently, I have had little recognition, responsibility, or advancement, and there had been a great deal of physical labor involved in my assignments.

My volunteer work gives me a chance to be useful, even in a small way, in the cause of elevating standards of education. However, most of the work is clerical—keeping up correspondence and records.

My education has contributed everything to the shaping of my tastes, to the choice of my hobbies and to my general outlook. Except for my brief teaching career, it has contributed little to my line of work. I never dreamed that opportunities for work in my field would be so few and, in terms of variety, challenge, and responsibility, my expectations have not been realized.

Being a woman has been a handicap in my work. As a man, particularly with a graduate degree, I might have been given supervisory posts, but as a woman, not even two degrees has been considered sufficient. I have, however, become absorbed in my recent assignment, and I am not sure that I would leave my present job for a college teaching position. My excellent undergraduate and graduate instruction have prepared me to cope with difficult assignments. But a specialization in Greek and Roman studies which is not accepted in the business world and the lack of a specialization that is has hampered my progress. In addition, the fact that I desire to remain with my family has limited all my activities to New York City, where there are few opportunities to teach Latin and Greek.

In a free society, all women ought to be able to rise as high as their aims and abilities will take them. Educational and career opportunities ought to be available to all on a fair, competitive basis. I have never married but I believe a married woman's first obligation is to her family. However, when time permits, as it usually does, she should be encouraged to study and work to reach her maximum personal growth, as a part of her obligations to herself, and her country.

SUMMARY

Certain strands run through the lives of the women whom we have classified as recasters. Some women mature slowly. While they are in college they are unable to clarify the kind of work they prefer to do, or even broadly, the kind of life they want to follow. Nevertheless, they must make some kind of decision, if only to proceed to the next stage of the educational ladder. Later, when they have acquired some understanding about their own values and goals, these women find it necessary or desirable to make changes in their initial plans.

Every individual undergoes experiences that either tend to confirm and reenforce his original plans and strengthen his initial goals, or which call his plans and goals into question so

that he must recast and reshape them. Many of those who become recasters are women who find through experience that
their initial planning does not yield the satisfactions they had
anticipated; for others, the circumstances in which they find
themselves make it impossible for them to pursue their original
plans. They want to, or have to, become recasters.

Marriage and children are sometimes precipitants to recasting. The changes brought about by marriage and the raising of
a family lead many women to alter their plans. Some do so
more or less under their own momentum; others have to in
order to remain in control of their lives.

This leads us to the concluding observation that, just as it
requires strength and foresight to plan one's life, so it requires
additional strength and perception to recognize that one's original plans are no longer satisfactory. At such a juncture, those
with vigor and purpose are able to recast their plans.

The Adapters

The recasters demonstrate flexibility in adjusting their plans when they are faced with new circumstances or conditions. The adapters make a way of life out of this quality. From the start of their planning they adopt open strategies in order to cope with the many possible conditions and circumstances that they expect to encounter. They have sufficient prevision to realize that the pattern of their adult existence may be subject to repeated and important alterations. Thus, unlike many of the recasters, they often avoid committing themselves to any particular goal too early or too firmly.

Yet the adapters are not fatalists. They are realists. When they encounter the necessity to alter their plans and actions, their approach to life allows them to make rather small changes, in contrast to the more radical shifts characteristically made by the recasters. The adapters, having less ambitious and less firmly fixed objectives, find it easier to compromise. It is relatively easy for them to reduce or to modify their aspirations.

A question that remains open is whether their avoidance of firm occupational and life commitments is primarily a reflection of their weaker involvement in interests and values or whether it reflects a deliberate strategy. Many adapters seem deliberately to have decided that, since life is fraught with uncertainty and contingencies, it is wise to avoid too early or too firm a commitment to any single track or approach.

Many of the adapters pursue their education to the point of achieving the doctorate, but this does not commit them irrevocably to a particular career or life plan as it seems to for many planners and, at first, for many recasters. The adapters convey the impression of being more relaxed individuals who are less dedicated to accomplishing specific occupational and life goals. Therefore, they are not unduly disturbed if their original direction has to be altered because of new circumstances, usually marriage and a family.

There is one further quality to their lives that warrants attention. The shifts, adjustments in aspirations, and the compromises that they make are easier for them because they seem to know from the outset that life is made up of a galaxy of pluses and minuses. While many regret that they are unable to carry through their initial plans, they feel that they have lost little from altering them. In fact, some even gain from a shift. While they might, for instance, forego some of the satisfactions that they anticipated receiving from working full or part-time, they recognize that these might be more than compensated for by the satisfaction derived from devoting themselves exclusively to their husbands and children. The adapters do not find their way of life burdensome.

Although adapters are generally prepared to make adjustments in all areas of their lives, most find that modifications are necessary in only certain spheres. The women in this group tend to follow a pattern of adaptations in one of three ways. Some may modify their work commitments either in response to the needs of their families or because of employment restrictions. Some may withdraw from work entirely for long periods, if not permanently, in order to attend to their children and to their homes. And some make adjustments in their family responsibilities in order to pursue their careers. However, in none of these instances are their actions as radical as those of the recasters. The adapters do not usually change their goals; they change their methods of achieving them. Most of the recasters suddenly discover that it is a woman's prerogative to change her mind. The adapters knew it all the time.

MODIFICATIONS IN WORK

While many adapters look forward to working and some contemplate pursuing careers, when they find that marriage interferes with their original occupational intentions they are prepared to modify their work goals accordingly.

For some adapters a husband and children means that they spend less time at work than they originally contemplated in order to devote more hours to their family's needs. For some women, this means occasional rather than continuous work. It may also mean a reduction in weekly hours of work or a change from full-time employment to free-lancing.

Other women may make modifications in their work because employers will not hire two members of the same family. Sometimes, this means a change in the type of work they do or in the employer for whom they work. For example, an anthropologist may change from university research to museum work; a college teacher may undertake independent research.

Some women modify their occupational patterns because of the mobility necessitated by their husband's work. Since they must move frequently, these women find that they do not remain in one location long enough to pursue a career systematically.

There is another group who decides that, on balance, it is better to modify their working plans quite substantially in order to devote their free time and energies directly to helping their husbands in their careers. While they might like to continue with their own work, they are not so determined in their own goals that they cannot put their personal plans aside. Some husbands need assistance; others welcome it even if they could do without.

Still another type of work modification is made by women who, because of responsibilities at home, find it difficult or impossible to work at a level that uses their full skills, for example, teaching at college level, but who are able to keep their footing in the world of work by taking a position lower in the job hierarchy, one which requires less preparation and time, such as that of a high school teacher.

These women know that they are dealing with total life situations in which compromise is their best answer to irreconcilable challenges.

Freda Lowe

My attitude toward women's work in general has been influenced by two migrations—from Germany to Belgium when I was 14, and from Belgium to the United States when I was 19. As a result of this unsettled life, my family and I felt that it was essential for a woman to be able to support not only herself, but her family as well, should it be necessary.

My parents attended graduate school in Germany, where my father was a lawyer and my mother a physician. My mother worked continuously (with many interruptions whenever we were sick) and enjoyed her work as a doctor. Occasionally, she was forced to undertake other work because of financial need. It was considered essential that my older sister and I get as much education as possible, but my mother's occupation did not influence me in the choice of mine. My

parents believed that women are no different from men as far
as education and work are concerned and so did I. Their education was an important factor in convincing my sister and me
of the desirability of college and graduate education, but their
particular fields never enticed us. Their financial position was
so bad that we got an education in spite of their inability to
help us. My sister is now a housewife.

I attended secondary school and art school in Brussels and,
after coming to the United States, entered Cornell University,
where I needed only two years to acquire my B.A. I received
financial help from a refugee organization which paid for my
tuition and later gave me an interest-free loan for my first year
of graduate work. My early goals had been painting and then
philosophy. But the invasion of Belgium during World War
II, when I was 19, very much influenced me to study in the
social sciences, since I believed then that wars are caused by
economic factors, and I felt I had to understand them. I rejected painting because I wasn't good enough, and philosophy
because I believed that an understanding of economics, rather
than philosophy, would help to prevent wars.

My major at Cornell was French, a carryover from my Bel-
gian training, but I had already become committed to economics before graduation and, after leaving Cornell, I took a position as a junior statistician for a large bank in New York.
While working there, I began to take graduate courses at Columbia, since I had always expected to do graduate work if I
had the opportunity. The intellectual atmosphere at home created the incentive, and fellowships, scholarships, and the opportunity for part-time work made it possible. The following
year, I left my job in order to work full-time for my M.A. and
continued in full-time study for the next three years. I received my master's degree in 1948, and the following year I
became part-time assistant in economics at an Eastern woman's
college to help finance additional study. I left after a year in

order to prepare for my Ph.D. orals and, after passing them, became an instructor at the same college.

In 1951, I was married to a fellow economist and went with him to a coeducational college in the South where he had received a teaching appointment. Institutional regulations barred husbands and wives from teaching at the same time *except* in emergencies. There were constant emergencies so that I taught most of the time, but the college took advantage of the fact that I had no other employment possibilities in that area and paid me even less than they paid unmarried women whose training and ability were similar to mine.

In 1960, the year I was granted my Ph.D., my husband was appointed to the faculty of the University of Chicago and, after we moved, I was offered a job as assistant professor at a suburban college. However, after a year I found the commuting too difficult and spent the next year engaged in independent research. In 1962, we moved to a Western city and I became an assistant professor at a local university, since I enjoy teaching and it was close to my home. However, it turned out to be far more difficult to teach these students than any others I had ever had. As a result, I had no time for my research. Therefore, at the end of the academic year, I left and I now devote myself to research and the study of mathematics.

I am satisfied with my choice of economics as my field, and I enjoy teaching subjects when I feel the students need my help, although I hate grading papers. I have not learned how to prevent wars but I am now extremely interested in the problem of the economic expansion of underdeveloped countries. My experiences compare favorably with my expectations, although they are somewhat different from what I expected. In a way, that makes my present activities fall somewhat short of expectations since conclusions are reached only after a lot of work. But I never dreamed that I would enjoy teaching so much until I actually tried it.

The obstacles I encountered when I was looking for work were substantial. Some organizations do not hire women at all for certain jobs, and most, in my experience, pay a woman less than a man with the same ability. Married women have a still harder time, especially in my field, college teaching. Most colleges are in small one-college towns. Since my husband is a college teacher, we need two positions in the same town, or within commuting distance since many colleges do not employ husband and wife, and there are few locations in the United States, except in the big cities, where two Grade A colleges are close together.

When I was young I thought marriage involved compromises, but not problems. The main compromise I envisioned was that I would want to stay home with my children until they were about 4 years old so that I, myself, could influence their early development. I have no children and the primary compromise my husband and I have had to make, since we both want to teach in colleges, involves restrictions as to location because of widespread nepotism rules. Yet, having the same vocation allows us to share our professional interests in addition to everything else. This sharing has added a beautiful facet to our marriage.

In general, I believe that higher education is very desirable for women who have the interest and ability to pursue it. Most women, I believe, should interrupt their careers while their children are small. But many find life relatively empty after the children are grown, and would be far happier if they could then resume an occupation that is as absorbing and satisfying as raising a family. The husbands, too, would be happier if their wives were not bored. In addition, women who return to their careers at this stage of their lives would make a far greater contribution to society if, instead of engaging in volunteer activities or taking relatively unskilled jobs, they could do work that would make full use of their abilities.

Doris Martin

My parents were largely self-educated; they emigrated to the United States after completing grade school, my father at a yeshiva in Lithuania and my mother at an elementary school in Rumania. Since they were unfamiliar with American mores and institutions, the guidance they gave their children primarily concerned general attitudes. They put much stress on education for their daughters as well as for their sons. They were altogether permissive about the decisions we made with regard to education, work, and marriage, but their broad respect for education strongly influenced me. This was especially true of my father, who was a self-employed photographer. My mother's only work experience was as my father's assistant; since his studio was in our home, this did not take her into the outside world. Her working in this way had no effect, really, on my decisions.

We lived in Troy, New York, where I was born in 1924. I entered Russell Sage College as a non-resident student when I was 16. My first vocational aim was social work, but I had changed to research and college teaching in sociology by graduation because of my reading and study in those fields as an undergraduate. While I was in college, I worked for a while in a social work agency. This had a negative influence in that I became convinced that I needed much more education and experience at various activities before I could even consider doing social work.

My interest in sociological theory with the vague notion of doing research and college teaching led me to enroll at Columbia for graduate work after receiving my A.B. in 1944. When I went to graduate school I did not expect to be married for some time. This expectation changed quickly, and 2 years later, before finishing my master's, I married another graduate student. This cut short my studies, since I had to go to Cambridge, for my husband was studying for his Ph.D. in French at Harvard and I had to work full-time to support him while he studied. Without the veterans' benefits which were available after World War II, my husband would not have been able to pursue graduate study. In fact our marriage at that time perhaps would not have been possible without those benefits.

In Boston, I was employed as a supervisor of interviewers for a public opinion research organization, since I had a related background in sociology. At this time and at later periods, I had some difficulty getting a job since I was "over-educated" for most and "under-educated" for others. Many employers took the former position, although I was willing to do the job. I found that employers hesitated to employ a woman, and especially a married woman, for a position of any responsibility. For more routine jobs, they believed that with my education and training I would quickly become bored (with such routine), and they again hesitated to hire me. However, working at various kinds of jobs with various people gave me confidence in my flexibility and competence in dealing with many different situations. When the polling concern went into bankruptcy in 1948 following the election, I took a job as a technical typist at a Harvard research lab.

I had abandoned, for a while, the thought of additional graduate work, but I left this job after a year to do graduate work in elementary education at Boston University, since I had a year which I could devote to study and I was interested in teaching children. I thought that I would be thus prepared to work at something I liked, whatever my husband's choice of position after he completed his graduate work. I thought of this as fulfilling requirements for a job rather than as graduate work in its fullest sense. Teaching children seemed to be the most feasible work in a small college town where my husband's work would probably take him. I returned to my technical typist job the following year after getting my M.Ed., since the surroundings were convenient and pleasant.

In 1951, my husband took a job at Bates College and I taught school locally. The school principal with whom I worked strongly confirmed my interest in public education. I took a year off in 1954 hoping to have a child; I taught piano and remedial reading and served as piano accompanist during this period. I did not have a child and I intended to return to teaching the following year, but we went to Princeton for a year where, instead, I became an assistant to a social psychology research group while my husband was a visiting lecturer.

In 1956, my husband became an associate professor of French at Temple University, and at my husband's urging I became a student of school psychology at the University of Pennsylvania. After my teaching experience and my work in psychology at Princeton, the move to Philadelphia made possible study and work in an area which combined my interest in public education with further work in psychology. Without my husband's aid, this graduate work would have been very difficult. He supported and encouraged me during these studies.

Ever since my 3 years of graduate study, I have been employed as a school psychologist in a suburb of Philadelphia. I took this job because it was broadly defined and I respected the people I was to work with. I get great satisfaction from seeing teachers and sometimes parents change their perception of children and thus their relationships with them, bringing about observable improvement in a child's learning and behavior. However, in this type of work, there is difficulty in ameliorating problems which spring from complex family situations and at times, when frustration is high, I contemplate going back to teaching, where I can work more directly with children—and not only with children who have troubles.

While I did switch my area of concentration, I don't think I would or could have gone directly to school psychology, which I am now engaged in. My early theoretical interests were necessary to my later work. My formal education was of course crucial to my "way of life," although I suppose that during my undergraduate and early graduate school years, I thought primarily of being concerned with theoretical matters and did not altogether anticipate my more recent absorption in practical affairs. I am still working on my doctoral dissertation and intend to complete it soon.

Since my marriage I have at all times been deeply interested in and concerned with my husband's work. At times I regret that because of my full-time work I cannot be of more help to him, both directly and in easing domestic arrangements. I also enjoy cooking and decorating my home and should like to have more time for this. I engage in no volunteer activities, although I am a member of professional associations. During my leisure, I play chess and devote much time to music—playing the piano, listening to music, and attending concerts. From childhood on, music has been a very important part of my life. I studied music formally for some 12 years and have always kept up my serious interest. I had, at times, thought of a career in music, but never seriously pursued it as a full-time interest, partly because I felt I did not have enough talent and partly because my other interests were equally strong and in many ways more practical.

The question of the value of a non-specific liberal arts education is easily answered. Sex is irrelevant here. The development of perspective in one's thinking which begins with study of the ideas crucial to our civilization has equal relevance for the person who is to be occupied primarily with a family and for a person who is to pursue a career. The question of graduate education for women is more complex and probably must in the end be answered on an individual basis. It is difficult in our society for a woman in her early twenties to think single-mindedly about a career. For too many, perhaps, graduate education is a stopgap until marriage and the raising of a family. Given the already existing strain on graduate facilities in the good graduate and professional schools, the common reluctance of such facilities to take women students seriously is understandable. Even if a woman completes her graduate training, it is likely that this training will have become obsolete or that her interests will be changed before she is in a position to pursue a career. One alternative is for women to think of postponing graduate training until serious concentration on such training is possible. "Going back" to school is difficult, though if such a course were to be "institutionalized" in our academic system, it could perhaps be made more feasible for more women. In some fields, if more part-time employment were made available, it might become more possible psychologically for a young woman to think seriously about her career from the start. Society, too, would have to change its largely ambivalent attitude toward part-time employment, though this is perhaps beginning to happen in reaction to the romanticized "natural childbirth," "happy family" ideal which prevailed following World War II. (This, in turn, had seemed to me a reaction to the intense and rather ridiculous feminism of earlier decades.)

I feel that my own hesitations, twistings, and turnings in my commitment to a career came out of a feeling that my first commitment was and would always be to my husband. Even now when I am fully engaged in a career, this is still basically true. If, for example, my husband were to be offered a job opportunity which necessitated a change in my job, I would not hesitate to make such a change. On the other hand, if such an opportunity arose for me, requiring a change for him, I would not consider it.

Another psychological obstacle which I and probably many

other women faced in seriously pursuing a career is that a dependent and protected position is the path of least resistance. Society says that a man must earn a living and an intelligent man must become engaged with the world—of ideas or of people—outside his family. No such demands are made on women, and to choose such engagement and its difficulties takes strong will and determination indeed. Yet, for myself and for those of my acquaintances who have finally chosen to work, satisfactions have been many, and for me and for others, too, marriages have seemed to become stronger as a result.

WITHDRAWAL FROM WORK

The family-oriented planners look forward to following the classic pattern that dictates a woman's withdrawal from work after the birth of her first child. Many adapters also follow this pattern, but they do so more in response to their own and their families' needs than because of an earlier plan. However, since they are always prepared to make adjustments in their lives, their homemaking does not have the quality that it would assume if they had to wrench themselves away from careers. Then, they would be recasters.

On the contrary, the adapters who withdraw from work are women who, while originally directed toward training and practice in the fields of their choice, can accept with equanimity the fact that children turn their thoughts away from work. It is not that they feel that the place of *every* mother is in the home. They have simply decided that *their* place is there, at least temporarily.

But since they are adapters rather than planners, the question of withdrawal cannot be decided uncritically. Other decisions remain open. How long should a mother stay at home—

until her youngest child enters nursery school, elementary school, high school, college? Different mothers have different answers.

There is a related question. Should the length of time that a woman stays away from the labor market be decided at least in part by her long-range plans? If so, how long can she afford to break her ties to work? Once again the answer depends on whether she has reasonably strong pulls to work and looks forward to returning to employment, and upon the nature of her field of specialization and level of skill. A woman who teaches English in high school and who is somewhat ambivalent about returning to her position faces a different problem from the scientist who has completed her work for the doctorate and who knows that her knowledge and skills may become obsolete if she stays away for even a few years.

Of critical importance in making this decision for many women is the attitude of their husbands. Some men insist that their wives stay home and care for the children until they enter college; others are satisfied if their wives remain at home for shorter periods. A woman whose husband is in the same field may be helped by him to keep her skills from tarnishing and thus it will be easier for her to pick up her interrupted career when the opportunity offers. On the other hand, the husband may refuse to assist his wife's efforts to return to work.

There are critical variables outside of the family as well. Whether or not a woman withdraws from work, and for how long, is greatly affected by the availability of adequate domestic help and child-care facilities. There is no question but that many women would have resolved this problem differently had they been able to hire competent housekeepers or had they had access to well-run child-care facilities.

Another important external factor is the attitude and policies of employers. Many women might continue to work— even full-time—if their employers had a little more flexibility.

But if there is no willingness to adjust the hours of work or the timing of vacations to enable married women with children to meet the imperative demands of their families, many women have no option but to stop working, even if they prefer to continue.

The final factor which dictates whether mothers withdraw from work is highly individual; it is the amount of their physical and emotional energy. Some women can carry a much bigger load than others; they can live in the two worlds of home and job and discharge their responsibilities in each. But most women, especially if they have several young children, cannot cope with the strain, and must give up some part of their activity. And others choose not to exhaust themselves in the first place.

Theodora Eichler

Both of my parents were born and educated in Austria. My father was an industrial designer who had the educational equivalent of about 2 years at a technical school and my mother was a graduate of a gymnasium. They were married after they immigrated to the United States, and my mother worked as a secretary and translator until I was born. Thus, working after graduation from school seemed the normal course of things to me.

My parents respected education and "learning," though my mother originally felt college was unnecessary for a girl. When I showed aptitude, however, she went along with my desire for higher education, and my parents, though not well off, willingly paid for it. They showed pride in my scholastic achievements and advised me to finish my Ph.D. and work for a few years before marriage, partly to gain experience in the world outside, partly so that my education would not be "wasted." They regarded marriage, once made, as "for keeps" and as a full-time career. The influence of these attitudes is subtle and difficult to evaluate, but without my parents' support, I would have found it difficult to acquire higher education no matter how determined I was.

I was born in Philadelphia and entered Bryn Mawr College in 1942, when I was 16 years old. I was very interested in biology and chemistry and decided as a freshman to work in some field that would combine these interests. I eventually majored in chemistry and by the time I graduated, I had decided to plan for a career in biochemistry. I was a dean's list student at college and received a fellowship for graduate study at Columbia. I had considered studying mathematics, but rejected it because at the time I seemed to enjoy chemistry more and because opportunities for a career in math were more limited than they are now. I also felt, vaguely, that my preparation in math might not have been quite adequate for advanced work. I decided on graduate work because of intense interest in my subject, my love of learning, and the desire to prepare for a professional career at a fairly high level in my field of interest.

I worked each summer during my undergraduate years at various jobs including playground direction, laboratory assistance, and tutoring. These helped finance my studies and gave me work experience in my field. My family's poor finances would have hindered the pursuit of graduate studies without my fellowships and part-time work in my department.

I was married to a fellow student after one year of graduate study and continued for another year, receiving my M.A. in 1948, at which time I had completed all my course requirements for the Ph.D. I could not complete my doctorate because when my husband completed his Ph.D., he found a job in another city and I was obliged to take over the care of his four-year-old child by a previous marriage.

Since that time I have been serving solely as a housewife and mother. My husband's career has necessitated frequent changes of residence, both intra- and inter-city, making it very difficult for me to establish a niche in any one location, or if it had been established, to pursue it. Except for contributing a chapter to a textbook written by my husband, I have been prevented, so far, from pursuing my career. At present, we live in Missouri. My husband travels and is absent for weeks at a time as an executive in a chemical firm. This increases my home responsibilities. He is not against outside work for me, but he has not actively encouraged it. When in graduate school, I was aware of problems involved in combining family and career, but I did not consider these insurmountable (more idealism than realism). The combination turned out to be particularly difficult because of frequent changes of residence, presence of small children, lack of availability of competent help, and because successful work in chemistry requires laboratory work.

I now have four children ranging in age from 1 to 18 years. Their needs are the dominant influence in my life; they require my presence at home almost continually when infants, the greater proportion of the time during preschool years, at least after school during school years, and again almost continually during the summer. This, plus the continued need for supervision during high school years and the lack of availability of intelligent and competent mother substitutes, seems to preclude pursuit of a full-time outside career and makes even a part-time one very difficult under present employment conditions. This also has prevented further work toward the completion of my thesis. Obsolescence of knowledge during the years spent at home multiplies the difficulty.

Though my husband now earns about $20,000 a year (before taxes), I have household help only once a week and have become expert at all manner of trades, including cooking, accounting, plumbing, serving, carpentry, gardening, painting, cleaning, hostessing, wallpapering, and personnel management. In fact, I have little doubt that I could probably out-Spock Spock, out-report *Consumers Reports,* and out-handyman *Better Homes and Gardens' Handyman!* Three of my children take serious music lessons and the cost of these and of keeping the family well supplied with books and records, plus all the familiar costs which make up living expenses—housing, taxes, maintenance, furniture, clothing, car, husband's professional society dues, food, and savings in the form of investments and insurance—leave me no choice but to meet most of the labor demands myself.

I have taken university courses in Russian for the enjoyment of the intellectual challenge, in consideration of the possibility of part-time employment in translation, and because of the desirability of knowing Russian in light of the present-day world political situation. I sometimes wonder whether mathematics might not have been the wiser choice of majors, because further work in it can more easily be carried on at home, but I question whether this really would have made much difference, because effective work in either biochemistry or mathematics would require much time for the necessary continuity in study and concentration.

Homemaking has many satisfactory aspects for me. There are the creative ones, such as designing an esthetically pleasing environment in which to live, and, above all, creating a new life, nurturing it, watching it grow and develop under one's guidance and care. There are also the emotional aspects involved in the shared experiences with others, the deep intimacy of the relationship with a small infant, the feeling of rediscovering the world through the eyes of each child, the awareness of the constant renewal of life which amounts to a rejuvenation. And, though facts and figures get rusty, the habits of a mind trained to think analytically, to evaluate, to synthesize are not lost but simply reapplied to different situations. The woman who graduates from her specialized training to homemaking is in same category as the physicist who graduates to administrative vice-president. He, too, is lost to physics, but his trained habits of mind are reapplied in his new work. In the case of women, the lowliest chore, such as deciding from observations, experiments, and stated information on labels what kind of wax is best for the kitchen floor, benefits.

The major flaws in my homemaking role include the endless repetition of monotonous chores and of exhortations to the older children; the sense of isolation; the lack of appreciation, recognition, and respect for one's efforts; the fragmentation of time, preventing concentration of effort on any matter of interest; and the obvious low esteem in which homemaking is generally held.

I have often engaged in various types of volunteer activity. For example, when we lived in Tulsa, I was on the board of the League of Women Voters. In Winnipeg, I was instrumental in preparing a special PTA brief for a city-wide committee on the Dominion school curriculum. Now, in Missouri, with a young infant, I spend most of my time at home. I did find the volunteer work to be an outlet for creative urges and to be intellectually stimulating. I enjoy contact with like-minded people, the sense of purpose, accomplishment, and progress, and the recognition of one's work. But committee work often involves frustration, and voluntary service is frequently just "busy work" and inefficient, thus necessitating the devotion of an excessive amount of time.

It should be borne in mind that many women develop new interests in volunteer and community work over the years and do not choose to start over again in their previous professions. Such work can be a most satisfactory outlet for creative impulses and the urge for self-expression and, at the same time, fill a much needed social function—after all, where would our symphony orchestras be without the backing and dedicated efforts of such women in fund-raising, serving on boards of directors, and, more subtly, providing the social setting in which such community enterprises flourish?

When time allows, I enjoy many leisure-time activities. My favorites are color photography, reading, listening to classical music, trying to play the piano, and studying ballet for enjoyment and exercise. I also like to swim, ski, skate, hike, and play tennis. Certain household activities, undertaken largely out of necessity, give creative satisfaction. These include dressmaking, gardening, carpentry, and interior decorating.

I have begun to think of the future and the past. The past, though it seems like yesterday, is 10 years ago. Advances in my profession have left me hopelessly behind; employers do not hire and begin to train married women in their middle or late thirties, with no experience, for positions commensurate with their abilities. There are few part-time jobs available with any sort of responsibility, certainly none in biochemistry, and there are few refresher courses available except in large university areas. The demands of household and children are still very great and would not allow any more than a part-time job, while 10 years hence, gratifying and useful full-time work might be possible but be even less available than now. Then, too, the family might at any time have to move again, and employers could hardly be blamed for being reluctant to hire and try to train such temporary help. So I drift, too often into a deadly routine of what has been called "circular puttering" —volunteer work of the most menial type, committees which, when disinterestedly dissected, reveal themselves as dedicated to producing nothing more than more unnecessary work under the guise of bettering community life. There is only one occupation open—teaching—and not everyone is suited to that.

I consider that the contributions of my formal education to my life are indirect; it determined the educational level of the man I married, the income level at which my family lives because of my husband's educational level, and, most significantly, the type of intellectual environment which I provide for my children.

But higher education fails the woman by preparing her for only one career, that of a professional man. This failure is made apparent by the problems of adjustment she often encounters when making the abrupt change from ivory-towered scholar to homemaker. The problem, as I see it, is one of redefining the purpose and approach of higher education; of readjusting prevailing attitudes and values with respect to the function of women in general and educated women in particular; and of guidance at the undergraduate level. The traditional ivory-tower approach in undergraduate years is particularly unsuited to women because of the atmosphere of cloistered unreality it lends. I think every girl should be required to take some type of "vocational seminar" in her junior or senior year. This might consist of talks and discussions about the position of women in today's society and particularly about professions. This should go far toward helping young women to acquire a sense of identity and a realistic appraisal of the problems likely to confront them upon embarking on whatever course they may choose after graduation.

Certainly, my experiences are quite different from what I expected when in school, which has made adjustment quite difficult and frequently accompanied by disillusionment and disenchantment. On the other hand, I did not expect the deep sense of fulfillment which accompanies childbearing and nurturing. This provides the supreme creative outlet for a woman and is the most important function of her life. The creation of a new life is a process next to which all other forms of creative expression pale; writing, painting, composing, whatever it may be, are but feeble substitutes. These points were brought home to me by a chemist friend whose children are in the care of an

illiterate South American woman while she is in the laboratory. At the time she was writing day and night to finish a
paper for publication before someone else "beat her to it," I
was then expecting a baby and my reaction could be worded
as follows: "Why should I as a woman expend so much energy
on a job which some man could do just as well when here
there is a job for me which no man could do at all and which
no one else could do as well?" It is too bad that this truth is
not more generally perceived.

Since housewifery and motherhood is the full-time occupation of nearly half the adult labor force, and many of these
women, like myself, have been highly educated and trained in
some special field of study and are not using their abilities in
any professional way, I think it is important to consider why
such valuable material and training is so often apparently
wasted. In an indirect way, it is not being wasted. Since the
mother, today, is the one most responsible for the education
and general rearing of children, the effect on the next generation of her tastes, critical abilities, and type of reading she provides must be obvious. Her own education may bear fruit only
in the next generation, a kind of second derivative effect.
Whoever said, "Educate a man, and you educate a man; educate a woman, and you educate a family," had a valid point.

However, this does not answer the question of why, in these
so-called emancipated days, most women are still unable to
utilize their talents and training *directly* within their speciali-
ties, if only in a small way.

In the first place, when a woman marries, she usually expects
and intends to have children, and this means that her interests
and career must immediately become secondary to those of
her husband, upon whom the main burden of supporting the
family will fall. The family will therefore be located in a community where career opportunity is greatest for him, not for
her. In fact it may be non-existent for her, particularly if she

has married immediately upon leaving school and has never
had a chance to work at her specialty before becoming involved in the responsibility of home and new babies in a new
and unfamiliar environment. She is, then, completely dependent on her husband's income, which will be none too large
since he, too, is just starting out. The demands placed on her
time and energy by children, by the sheer necessity of keeping
the house clean and up to today's high standards, by her husband's rising status in the social and political strata of the organization he works for, and by the social and civic duties the
community expects its members to perform are simply enormous. The analogy of the drowning man clinging to a straw is
a good one; living becomes a matter of trying to cope with
each day as it comes and there is no time even for thoughts of
either the future or the past.

Suddenly, five years have gone by, then six, eight, ten. By this
time some of the children are in school and the family may have
moved several times. The husband's income has risen, as have
the cost of living and the demands of his job, his status, and his
outside activities in professional societies, which increase his
prestige and thereby further his career. This, of course, is
good for the family. The wife can now probably afford household help at least once a week, possibly more, but the higher
cost of living and of educating children in her own image and
her own scale of values prevent the wife from hiring this
help. For example, when a choice must be made between
music lessons for her children and a gardener who probably
charges much more than the music teacher, the wife does the
gardening herself; when a choice must be made by her husband between going to a professional meeting and painting the
bathroom, she paints the bathroom; professional painters
charge prohibitive prices and the money will buy a desk for
Johnny, etc. In a sense, it is the housewife who pays the price
for everyone else's high standard of living.

In this way, even in this so-called emancipated age, does the tyranny of a woman's biology still subdue her potential for intellectual attainment and her capacity for making a genuinely creative contribution to an advanced field of study in a professional way. Nor is there any foreseeable manner of getting away from the fact that while a man is carving his career, a woman is taking care of the future of the race, and obviously, with the future of the race at stake, it would not be desirable to get away from it. However, after 15 or 20 years, when she is in her forties, a woman is able to begin another career, which could keep her usefully and productively occupied for another 30 or 40 years—I submit that this is a human resource which is today largely not being conserved, probably because it is available for the first time in history and we don't as yet know what to do with it.

I think some of the solution lies, first, in continuing to educate women in advanced studies and, second, in awakening the imagination of both universities and employers to the possible applications of their potential. Above all, what is needed is a bit of encouragement and an extended welcoming hand. The instinct to help others with very little expectation of financial reward or of public recognition is very deep-seated in a woman and an invitation such as "We've come up with a rather interesting little problem in our work lately, which we don't have time or resources to follow up right now; would you like to see what you can do with it on your own?" would make any scientifically trained woman drop the tea cup she's just been pouring and send her running forward. It's hard to estimate how much valuable work, now being left undone, could be accomplished by the available numbers of such women.

There is one other way of attacking the problem, and that is not to let it arise in its acute form in the first place. This can be done by means of a minor social change, namely, providing

well-run day nurseries on an extended scale and at nominal
cost, administered possibly by the departments of education.
This, of course, is the system which enables Russia to utilize
the educated talent of its women; its absence here is responsible for much loss of valuable talent which could be conserved
by freeing the mother's mind and hands two or three days a
week for work which furthers her own professional career.

There are other factors, less tangible, that may have a pro-
found effect. These are the personal factors: whether there is
much conflict within the family group, with other relatives,
with difficult children; whether the marriage is a happy one or
a constant source of anxiety; and what the husband's attitude
is—whether he is sympathetic and encouraging and willing to
make some sacrifices for the sake of his wife's interests, or
whether he tends to be indifferent, or even jealous of her ac-
complishments, or opposed on principle to her pursuit of
them. Another factor is the woman's own psychological state,
which is a conflict between feelings of guilt for having let
down the people who put so much into providing her education, and feelings of guilt for letting down her husband and
children by devoting too much time to outside interests; the
effect of such a conflict on personality must be detrimental
and a hindrance to constructive work of any kind. Still another factor is the feeling of inferiority which results from the
increasing unfamiliarity with subject matter that was once so
familiar and which comes with the realization that her training
is apparently no longer of any value to anybody, the feeling
that she is "just a housewife," an occupation which in our
complex society is certainly among the most exacting and
highly skilled trades anywhere, at least if there are children,
but which certainly does not rank among the high status professions in the public mind.

I favor a change of attitude, first, on the part of educators,
women themselves, and society in general, restoring homemak-

ing as a career to the position of dignity it once had, and, second, on the part of employers, in recognizing the assets of the mature, responsible, intelligent married woman. An awareness is needed on the part of all concerned of the importance of the educated homemaker to society because of the enormous influence she has on the next generation.

Presumably, a woman's creative urges could be satisfied and fully utilized by having a baby every year, as she was biologically meant to do, but this is obviously not practicable, and there must come a time, when she is through bearing her limited number of children, when she needs a substitute outlet for her creative impulses. The Radcliffe system, which offers grants to career-bent married women even to help defray the cost of household help, is a wonderful start, and should be made universal. Employers with a little imagination could make use of a great fund of talent, again by permitting flexible hours, home work, and contracting out work on an individual basis, i.e., utilizing a type of professional Kelly Girl system. Surely most employers must be conscious of the assets (as well as the liabilities) of the married career woman—her stability, resourcefulness, flexibility, willingness to make an effort—and surely, after years of experience in managing a household and family, she is something of an expert at coordination of effort and in human relations!

Beth Isaacs

My parents had a deep pride in educational achievement but *never* pushed me, and I ingested all their attitudes early—without special spoon-feeding. They were born in Russia and attended college in the United States, but only my mother graduated. She has been a junior high school teacher of English literature for over 35 years, and my father is a factory manager who is very proud of my mother's stature as a teacher. Teaching is my mother's passion and pride. She has pride in herself and in America to which she came as a small child in deep poverty. I was always impelled to excel in school, but whether this was due to my mother or not, only a psychoanalysis would tell. I do think that my parents' attitudes toward educational achievement always resulted in my reaching for the highest goals (Phi Beta Kappa in college, and desire for graduate study, for example). Although my parents had a deep commitment to family, marriage, and children, we had a sleep-in maid when I was young since my mother worked. I did feel that I would want to be home with my young children.

I was born in Detroit in 1928 and entered the University of Michigan in 1945. I was married during my sophomore year to a fellow student, and when he began graduate studies in mathematics at Columbia the following year, I transferred to Barnard, where I majored in economics and was graduated magna cum laude in 1949. My original goal at Michigan was to work in English literature, but when I met my future husband he suggested I go in for a more "scientific" career so, on whimsy, I switched to economics, planning to do research and teaching in that field. One important influence at that time was a professor at Barnard with whom I participated in a later-published study. She managed to combine teaching, research, and motherhood in a remarkable manner.

Since I wanted to be a research economist, graduate work was in the natural course of things. I seem to have an insatiable desire to continue learning new things and studying always. I was granted a fellowship for graduate study at Columbia after college graduation, and received my M.A. in 1951. Marriage did not affect my education except that we worked constantly to earn money for our schooling. During my second year of graduate work, I served as an assistant in the economics department at Barnard but, on receipt of an additional fellowship for the following year, I was forced to give up this work to comply with the rules on which the grant was based. I also served as a part-time assistant in the Columbia School of General Studies. These assistantships increased my positive feeling for an academic career in economics. All of my credits for the Ph.D. were completed and qualifying exams passed by 1952. All that had to be done was the thesis. However, my husband had obtained his Ph.D. and was leaving Columbia for postgraduate work at California Institute of Technology. Of course, I went with him. Any regrets? Not for what we've *had* together—but only for what *I* haven't completed and gone on with.

When I was at Columbia I learned how "disadvantaged" a woman can be. Because of her future "time-out" from work it is even more desperately necessary for a woman than for a man to receive lots of *practical training,* as a graduate assistant in teaching and research and as a lab assistant in the sciences. These jobs (in undergrad courses) were for graduate student *males.* Once I asked a professor for such a "practical assistantship" (I *had* scholarship money. It is not the lack of *financial* help I'm decrying. Columbia was more than generous to me in this way) and he said to me, "I can't, Beth. You're a *very* bright student but you'll have children and quit working in the field and not be publishing papers which redound to the credit and illustrious name of the university. So I will choose a male assistant." He was quite correct.

This is a dilemma for a university, but for a woman, too—and for society in the long run. Perhaps I'm being selfishly concerned for women, but I wish universities could give extra doses of attention to the women students (my thesis professor was away in Europe during the entire year I worked on my Ph.D. dissertation, after which time I had to leave Columbia to join my husband 3,000 miles away.) I know so many professors' wives embittered by too much intelligence, too much training, and no work life available because of interrupted graduate degrees. Or they lack solid *work* experience *during* the graduate period which could serve (even with the time interval due to family raising) as a foundation for job-seeking late in life. Watching my husband's work with his graduate students today, I am shocked by how *long* and *close* an apprenticeship for their future work is available and insisted upon, in comparison to what I found in this respect at Columbia.

My first child was born in 1952 and since then, the children (I now have three, aged 11, 8, and 5) and their needs and happiness have effectively shunted aside all my former work goals, although the inner desire to do creative research and teaching remains as a definite "ache" always. We moved around a great deal, in Europe for a year and in this country. Our place of residence has always been up to my husband and his work needs, and I've been delighted to see so much of the world as a consequence. Since 1957, we have lived in an Eastern university city where my husband is a professor of mathematics and a research project director. I had to decide whether being a full-time mother was more important than my work goals— and decided that nursing each baby for a year plus staying home with the young ones was more important for us all than the financially and spiritually unfeasible plan of my trying to work outside the home, especially with my Ph.D. uncompleted. At Barnard I thought women could conquer the world, have children, *and* be great professors. Now I feel that expectation surely shattered. To be a warm, loving mommy you've got to be home with your kids, not *perfect* with them, but with them, *enjoying* them. And this chunk of energy and time taken out of a woman's life is scarcely replaceable.

Think of the great production of good research by a man during these years. There is simply no "competing" possible. Also, if a woman wants to create a good marriage it is the labor of many years and much adaptation. Rarely can her husband reach pinnacles of erudite or intellectual fulfillment and productivity if she is busy shoving onward and upward too, at the same time. And if it does happen, perhaps they will end up strangers in a certain sense—not two richly complex, truly mated people in a deeply stable creative family environment.

I want my husband to be free to be as fine a scientist as he can. This means being home so he can run over to his office, any hour of the day or night, and when the children were younger it meant taking physical care of them myself so that if my husband *were* home he didn't have to be bathing or feeding a child but could relax at the piano or with a newspaper.

To create a safe, warm, free place in a senseless world of poised atomic threat is my great joy. Here is the Garden of Eden, where even serpents have a right to dwell—joy, sorrow, laughter, quarrels, yells—but still deep affectional bonds and a natural sense of belonging to each other and to our little world of garden, friends, children—home. I love my non-paying "jobs" as mother, teacher, and secondary-reinforcer, among others, but they give few satisfactions in terms of professional achievement.

I have engaged in volunteer work, spending a few hours a month in activities with such groups as the Civil Liberties Union and CORE. I also work for the Foreign Wives Club and like helping other people to be happy. It is good to make foreign visitors comfortable, interest them in American things, and find out about their countries. But I never do too much of such work so that it in any way interferes with my care of my children or husband. However, it has enhanced our interests and circle of friends. I also studied Russian for 2 years, since it seemed to me that it will be the great "science" language of the world, together with English, as well as the language of a people with whom we shall have to learn to live for the sake of the peace of the world. I have also been singing serious choral music in a community chorale and have assisted my husband in a research project on an irregular basis.

As the children grew older, without some outside work my sense of special usefulness as a mother declined a bit. A month ago I began work as a research assistant in economics on a half-time basis (20 hours per week). The job offered to me sounded like very interesting research, which would give me a chance to get back into economics on a professional level, and the possibility of part-time work. Since my youngest begins kindergarten this coming fall it seemed too fine an opportunity for creative work to let it slip. So far, I love being among professional adults as well as among all kinds of people; I never realized how limited was my contact with other adults during the day while I stayed at home exclusively. Also, I have a chance to initiate my own projects and to participate in exciting, socially meaningful, ongoing research. But if the children seem edgy because I've worked that day, it's upsetting and I have to be extra good to them just when I'm tired. Also, the status business of my non-Ph.D. condition sometimes is mildly annoying.

I'm not really sure I could have afforded to work before this. Household assistance, car expenses, and other costs for my 20-hour work week use up most, if not all, of my salary. My husband's attitudes about my working were dual. If I had taken a job which was beneath my educational level, he would have disapproved of my taking that time away from the children and himself, too. With a job full of creative opportunities, interesting work utilizing my training, he was in full agreement and is quite pleased about my new position. He has made it a point to do more things with and for the children to ease their adjustment to my being away part of the time now.

I value education, and people who learn and experiment and think, well above any possible material goal in life. I am married to a professor at a university and, in a certain sense, all my education has led to my present social world which is over-whelmingly university people and families, music, politics, *et al.* I'm sorry I haven't the Ph.D., but if I can do some good research without it, or can teach, perhaps (though this seems doubtful given the *rigid* insistence on the Ph.D. at universities), I shall be very happy. And certainly I would never wish to have been first a career woman and then a wife and mother. If my children are growing strong and beautiful in life, I am ego-centric enough to think it's because I stayed home and nursed them and held them and scolded them and smiled on them. If spending these past 10 years as homemaker has meant I shall never be "famous"—so, I'll never be "famous"; but I shall see my children grow into people I enjoy and like. If, as they need me less, I can begin to find a *rewarding* place in a working world, it is my pleasure and good fortune, and I shall be very thankful.

As for "women in general"—there is no "general." Chacun à son goût—et à sa fortune! Bravo to all the higher education a woman can get. It will make her a richer human being, a more intelligent citizen, even if sometimes a confused-about-her-goals woman. Some mothers whom I know, with Ph.D.'s, would be so miserable just "staying home" that it is a far bet-ter thing for themselves and their families that they should work, although if they are professors' wives they have rough sledding finding a job because of nepotism laws and such.

If a woman can make a career in a field like nursing, school teaching, or piano teaching, where she can be home with her children as soon as their school day finishes, she can perhaps most satisfactorily continue both homemaking and a career. I know some fine examples of this type of "solution."

This still doesn't answer the questions of what to do with the woman who has the potential or actual Ph.D. in a science, for instance. How to satisfy her work and family needs is a big problem. I know of another interesting aspect of this problem:

An example is a woman who got her Ph.D. 10 years ago, gave up work to raise her family, and now probably could easily get a job (with the magic degree, of course); however, her values about research and area of study have changed, and she's just not as sure her field is so all-fired important or interesting to go back to.

I can go on indefinitely ruminating, and providing many "case histories" personally known to me, but I am sure my themes have probably been sung over and over by women graduates. I do feel that getting a clear picture of the attrition of women's talents and abilities in our culture is a terribly important undertaking. On balance, my great desire to give time and attention to the children and house, and my great desire that my husband's scientific creative work should be as unhampered as possible, interfered with the realization of my career goals. But my intense love of learning and interest in my special field will contribute to any career I may now be commencing.

ADJUSTMENTS AT HOME

While most of the adapters find it easy to modify their career and work patterns in order to deal with the additional challenges of marriage and motherhood, some women make other adjustments. Work is such an important facet of their lives that they hesitate to surrender the satisfactions which they derive from it, even for a limited number of years. Confronted with difficulties and conflicts between work and home, this next group seeks to modify their home environment in the hope of finding a tolerable balance.

Those who have small families are of course better able to do so. Many women deliberately limit the size of their families because they realize that it is easier, in general, to provide adequate substitute care for one or two children than for four or five. Others do so because time off for rearing several children would interfere with their progress in work.

In addition to the size of one's family, the question of where one lives is important. Women may shun living in suburbia, for example, where there are few jobs for educated women and where commuting would add to the other burdens assumed by a working mother.

A more subtle factor is the amount of time that a woman believes she should devote to her husband and children and, in turn, their expectations of her. If a woman who wants to work also wants to meet all of her obligations as wife and mother—as defined by her non-working neighbors—then she may find herself trapped between her excessive expectations and the constraints of time, place, and energy. But the adapters in general have modest expectations and seldom have unattainable goals. The women who want to work may cut back on some domestic and family obligations but they usually are able to find sufficient time and energy to meet their overriding duties and desires.

The compromises that they are able to work out at home often are considerably eased by the understanding and considerateness of their husbands, sometimes of their older children. The fact that many men are willing to accept certain conditions at home—a less than spotless house, a limited amount of entertaining, the necessity to help with household chores and the care of the children—frequently represents the margin of difference between whether women can or cannot work. Many men believe that it is important for their wives to work, and are able and willing to make adjustments and compromises in order to enable them to do so.

These modifications, like those of all adapters, are *ad hoc* adjustments rather than the results of long-range planning. They meet the immediate needs of these women as they are confronted by new circumstances and they change as conditions change. Some women may alternate periods of adjustments at home with modifications at work, depending on the needs of the moment. There is no rigidity in their approach to life. They are ready to adjust to the changing scene.

Norma Allison

Both of my parents were born in Latvia and neither had any education beyond grade school. My father was a real estate agent in Brooklyn and my mother was continuously employed as a milliner because of the need for money to support the family. One might say that everything or most things about my childhood home pushed me toward something different. My mother always showed respect for and appreciation of the educated person. My father was against higher education, and although my mother was willing, she was not anxious (for financial reasons) for me to go to college. I fought to be allowed to go and worked to get myself through. I can't remember when I was not delighted with school.

I was born in 1914 and have one brother, now a salesman, who was born 10 years later. At the age of 18, I entered Brooklyn College, where I majored in chemistry. The first course in chemistry which I took in high school had driven out all previous devotion to history, my first love; from then on chemistry was my field of concentration. My teacher at that time made it my consuming interest. While at college, I had an assortment of jobs to help me through school including teaching English to the foreign-born, baby-sitting, knitting for pay, waiting on tables in a summer camp, and working for a WPA-type of project in botany. These experiences made me perhaps a little bitter; they reinforced my feeling that it should not be necessary to work so hard in order to "appreciate what you have achieved."

While I was in college I had planned to teach at the secondary school level, but later I hoped to do graduate work in biochemistry. However, after graduation in 1937, I didn't have the money for graduate school and I had to go to work in a business office. After losing my job 3½ years later, I dutifully registered with many employment agencies, but in 1940 nothing much happened. Unemployment insurance left me free to volunteer and that led to a job in a lab and to further education.

In 1941, I enrolled as a graduate student in biochemistry at Columbia, taking 12 points that year while working at various jobs to pay my way. I was permitted to enroll despite an interviewer who said: "I would rather take a mediocre man than a brilliant woman, because he'll continue to produce." I had a strong desire to work in this field, particularly with one of the professors in the department whose research fascinated me. I hoped to combine teaching with research at the medical school level. The following year I was employed at the College of Physicians and Surgeons as a part-time lab assistant; this made it possible for me to buy food and pay rent while I studied. When asked to work full-time in 1943 "since a war is on," I had to turn down this position because I couldn't go on with graduate work if I worked full-time.

I was married in 1943, one day before my husband joined the Air Corps. (I had known him for 6 years but had originally planned to earn my degree before I married.) When I found I could not combine a half-time job with a scholarship, I interrupted my graduate work at Columbia and joined my husband at his station in Atlanta. I arranged to take two courses at Emory and worked part-time as a lab assistant for one of the professors until my husband was transferred to Cal-

ifornia. I served as a teaching assistant in biochemistry at
Berkeley until my husband was mustered out of the army in
1946.

My only child was born that year. I resumed part-time graduate study at Columbia in 1948 with scholarship aid, while my
husband, who had acquired a Ph.D. in psychology, worked as
a university instructor. By 1951, I had completed my doctoral
requirements, and I received my degree the following year.
During the last 2 years of my graduate work, I took a job as a
teaching assistant in biochemistry at the NYU Bellevue Medical Center; this made it possible to finish my graduate work.
When I had received my Ph.D. I had a choice of two jobs: an
opportunity to work in a lab as a postdoctoral fellow on a
problem connected with cancer research, and an instructorship
in biochemistry at a medical school (which was supposed to
combine teaching with research possibilities). Since I enjoyed
both teaching *and* research, I accepted the instructorship. I
was also influenced by the fact that my daughter was very
young and the latter job left summers free. However, I sometimes feel that the postdoctoral fellowship might have spurred
me into better research efforts.

I'm sure I'd have tried to have another child if doing so
hadn't meant that a new Ph.D. would have to be put on ice.
At that time, when biochemists were in short supply, I tried to
get a job which would keep me away from my home only during teaching assignments. It could not be done in the New
York area.

I continued in this position for five years, until a colleague
who was offered the chairmanship of the biochemistry department at another medical school asked me to join his department as assistant professor. Since I had received no advancement in rank and very little increase in salary (from $3000 to
$4500), and since the atmosphere of the department did not
encourage research (i.e., only one staff member was engaged

in research, and the teaching obligation ran from September to the end of May, with no unencumbered block of research time), I accepted this offer. I am now a full-time associate professor. I can think of only one area in which the fact that I am a woman has brought me special assistance—the lifting of projection equipment, and carrying heavy books. On the other hand, my salary of $10,000 is less than that of *men* of the same period in rank in my own department receive.

Although I am not by any means a "hot-shot researcher," I get a great deal of pleasure out of my combined job of teaching medical students and doing research. I enjoy being in a laboratory. I enjoy teaching in the fall, but am usually quite happy when it is completed for the year by the end of January, and I can spend the remainder of the year in research. I expected to be able to contribute more to biochemical research than I have in fact done. Otherwise, things have worked out about as I anticipated. I occasionally contemplate going into a straight research job, especially around exam time, since I dislike preparing and marking examinations, but I haven't made the change, mainly, I think, because I enjoy the relative freedom of my job setup.

When I married during the period of my graduate studies, I knew it was obviously going to be rough to manage home and career with the small income generally available at that time, yet I was convinced it could be done with a cooperative husband. The high cost of decent domestic and child-care help, together with the increased income tax on combined family earnings, offset any financial gain during the early years of my professional work. Only as my salary increased did my work improve the economic status of our family, some 5 years after I had received the Ph.D.

I also enjoy our physical surroundings. I had not lived in a house until three years ago, when we moved to Westchester. I'm an apartment-born-and-bred New Yorker. Least gratifying is all the work connected with cleaning, cooking, laundering, and other housekeeping chores. My husband, who is now a full professor, has always been most cooperative about my work and, before I obtained the Ph.D., about my study needs. He feels that marriage is a fifty-fifty proposition and has always helped with our daughter and our house. When my daughter was young, I chose a job that made no demands on my summer time. Also, our move to the suburbs seemed wiser in view of her needs, although I hated it at first.

I don't engage in any active volunteer work, but when possible make financial contributions to causes I deem worthwhile. I am also a member of a professional association and attend three to four days of meetings a year. I have strong convictions regarding social and political action, but am not a joiner. My education shapes my activities almost entirely, except for "extra-curricular" interests, such as theatre and concerts. I would like to learn to work with silver and I used to think I could still learn to play the piano sometime before I die.

For me, education and the opportunity to use my education as a basis for work is absolutely essential. It would continue to be necessary no matter how my husband's status improved (he now earns about $15,000 annually). In general, I think education for women should be vigorously encouraged. I feel women should work at jobs which bring satisfactions. If, while children are young, their mothers could obtain part-time work in the fields of their interest, many more women might contribute meaningfully. The present situation makes it necessary for women to choose between a full-time job or none at all.

I think many women would make better mothers if they worked away from home. Too many educated women suffocate in the home situation, meeting minor crises with children 24 hours each day, never being exposed to intellectual stimulation. In spite of all that has been learned about child psychology, many frustrated females are emotionally unable to bring up their children well. If women worked away from home, as do their husbands, they might feel as relaxed as most fathers seem able to be with their children. Not being with a small child all day made it much easier for me to be reasonable and patient and understanding of her needs and her behavior. I admit that I curtailed other activities when she was very young so I could play with her. I might add also that I was often physically tired.

In my present job, I hear repeatedly about the wastefulness of admitting women to medical schools. The men drag out all kinds of statistics to show how few women doctors continue in medicine if they marry. Yet, few of the men are willing to consider making it possible for women doctors to have families *and* to continue working on a part-time basis. Surely, there is need for such work in schools, in clinics, in group medical practices and in other areas.

I feel that if educated women were *expected* to make work contributions just as educated men are expected to do, more of them would continue their careers. To the best of my knowledge, having a baby does not reduce the number of neurons in the thinking apparatus.

Tamara Newberry

When I was 4 years old, my parents were divorced and I never saw my father again. Both of my parents had attended graduate school and were writers, and my mother has worked continuously since her divorce both for the money and for the satisfaction. She got more of the latter than the former.

I was born in New York in 1924 and raised in Boston, where I attended a private progressive school from which I was graduated in 1942. I then entered Radcliffe, where I majored in

German, was elected to Phi Beta Kappa, and was graduated summa cum laude in 1946. During my senior year, I was president of the undergraduate association. In college, I envisioned a career in diplomatic work. I never knew my father at all, but I knew that he was an academic man, and, since my mother is a writer, I had always assumed that I would follow some sort of professional career. It never occurred to me that educated women did not work. I was also brought up to believe that only stupid women married and raised children. I had a lot of unlearning to do!

The summer following college graduation, I was married to a graduate student in chemistry. My mother was so strongly in favor of my "career" that she almost committed suicide when I decided to marry (I still believe she really meant this although she did not carry out her threat). She felt that I had sacrificed my life to my family and, while I did not fortunately, believe that nonsense, I think my having continued to study and work comes in part from never having seriously considered not doing so.

Immediately after our marriage, my husband and I went to Liberia, where we taught for 3 years, because we wanted to "improve" the world after the war. We taught English at a school for girls, attended largely by Liberian students. This experience overcame a prejudice on my part *against* teaching and made me decide that that was the career for me. The only way to learn how to teach (Teachers College to the contrary notwithstanding) is to teach.

I knew I would need graduate education to teach at the college level. Thus, at the conclusion of the employment contract and our return to this country in 1949, I applied for and received a graduate fellowship in African history at Columbia. Living for three years in Liberia, along with the special insights which I gained there, had made me feel that it would be both interesting and useful to enter this neglected field of specialization. My husband was appointed to the research staff of a chemical manufacturing firm, and resumed his Ph.D. preparation.

While abroad, I had given birth to a son in 1947. He attended nursery school while I attended graduate school. I received an M.A. in 1950 and continued my studies, so that by 1952 I had qualified for a Ph.D. My second child was born that year and I ceased my studies in order to care for my two children and to help my husband finish his Ph.D. in chemistry, which he received in 1955.

In 1954, I became an instructor of history at an Eastern women's college where I taught the required freshman course for a total of 9 hours a week. It offered part-time work that I could manage with care of small children, in contrast to other teaching possibilities in private secondary schools that would have been full-time. I remained there for 8 years and that institution's willingness to keep reappointing an instructor after the critical third year of up or out gave me confidence in my ability to progress in the teaching field. I had not expected to be able to get and hold a part-time college teaching job without a Ph.D., and I was fortunate that I was able to do so. My last salary was $4,300 a year. I had the typical teacher's gratification of converting an occasional student to the life of the mind, and the typical discouragement of failing to convince the many more.

In 1956, my third child was born, but I continued my part-time teaching. However, my children's needs stopped my work in the Ph.D. degree from 1952 to 1962. I have always felt able to do any two of the following: study, teach, run my home—but never all three. As there has been no question about the children, the other two have taken turns. I always managed a part-time teaching schedule by using nursery school as a baby-sitting service. I found that that way I did not feel guilty about neglecting the family. After my third child entered first grade in 1962, I changed from part-time work to full-time study when I received a graduate fellowship in the field of Near Eastern studies at an ivy league university. Since we live nearby and my husband is associated with the same institution as a research chemist, I am easily able to attend classes and use university facilities. If I had not been admitted here, there would have been a serious obstacle to my studying what I wanted in the time at my disposal. I estimate that I devote 45 hours a week to homemaking and 60 hours to my educational pursuits; the fact that I am at present a full-time graduate student dominates the schedule.

As an academic person, my husband believes that my work is interesting and important; as an extraordinary husband, he has helped me in every possible way, such as coming home if a child were sick and I couldn't come home, and overlooking sloppy housekeeping and casual cooking. He has always supported me so that I could work at part-time teaching instead of working for money. I never have paid attention to the amount of money I make or to what I pay for household help. My husband's salary is between $12,000 and $15,000 a year. Having a more cooperative husband than most, and better physical health and strength than most, I have been able to do what has really amounted to two full-time jobs for most of my adult life.

My experiences are closer to my earlier expectations than I had any right to expect; except for the long delay in getting my graduate degree (B.A. 1946, Ph.D. 1966, with luck) it has been much as I anticipated. I was utterly ignorant of both the satisfactions and burdens of having children, and learned a good deal about both. Seeing children grow and become independent and learn things they didn't know before is highly gratifying to me. When I started the M.A. with one 2-year-old, I had infinite ignorance of my role. When I started the Ph.D. (again), 13 years older, more experienced, with three children, 15, 10, and 6, there was full awareness of the implication of combining marriage and a career. In terms of career alone, I have accomplished very little; add three sons and husband, and I feel quite satisfied. Home has come first for 15 years, job second. My graduate education has determined virtually every aspect of my present life, from study to teaching and back again. I have no doubt that it will ultimately influence the views of the children in the family, though perhaps in unpredictable ways. I plan to return to college teaching after receiving my doctorate and to retire in 1981 or 1988. Then, if we have money and health—travel.

My outside activities have included work for PTA's, the Democratic Party, and interracial housing. I believe these have contributed to my career, insofar as activities involving social and political action have a definite bearing on the teaching of history. Yet, they're time consuming and mean time away from study. I enjoy skating, skiing with my family, reading, and entertaining.

I feel very strongly that the problems of emancipated American women have been far from solved. The middle-class prejudice, influenced by Freud and Dr. Spock, against women's working or leaving their children at all for anything has left women with a genuine dilemma. Will they become slaves to children and kitchen and allow their studies to fade and their minds to close? Or will they challenge the community's values, and work and suffer the accompanying guilt? Or will they compromise (as I did) with the consequent feeling that nothing is ever done quite completely or quite right?

Compromise has worked very well for me because of several very personal factors. The first was early home training which argued against becoming a hausfrau and for a career. The second factor has been the complete moral support and help of my husband. The third is physical health and energy. This leaves me now with a foot in the career door and with the opportunity to push it open and enter full-time work. However, there is little doubt in my mind that the really wasted human resource is the educated woman, and unless more intelligent women are encouraged to work with their minds without feeling too guilty about neglecting their children, we shall be losing their help in a natural and human endeavor and, what may be more important, they will feel frustrated and unhappy.

My generation (approaching 40) seems to me to be an in-between one: between the suffragette and the "trained-brain" generation and the post-war "be well adjusted, nurse your baby and plan your life around him" generation. Perhaps that is what has made a compromise life satisfactory to some of us.

Most of my women friends my age are now attempting to get back into some kind of professional work. Many have dropped it entirely for fifteen years and are frightened at the prospects of working again; others find their places taken by men, or younger or unmarried women. I think the major problem for educated women today is their tendency to feel guilty no matter what role they choose; I know of no sensitive woman who hasn't some sense of guilt. I do feel, however, that the climate of opinion is changing and has already changed somewhat; the Radcliffe Institute is an example of this.

If I had daughters instead of sons, I should attempt (hopelessly no doubt) to advise them to finish college at least before marriage; to work or do some graduate study before having children; to marry men who would encourage their personal (and not just family) development; and to consider part-time work, first in order to continue to be persons and not just mummies, and second in preparation for the day when home-keeping is no longer a full-time job. Having only sons, I feel that they will in the long run be happier married to such women.

SUMMARY

These are the qualities that run through the lives of the adapters. First, these women see their lives as subject to a high order of uncertainty and contingency. They allow for many possibilities with regard to marriage, children, place of residence, income, and work. They conclude that the sensible way to plan for contingencies is to realize in advance that their lives may be shaped one way or another, and to be in positions to live under whatever conditions they encounter.

Inherent in the adapter's relaxed stance toward her future are two characteristics: first, the traditional approach that a woman must accommodate herself to the needs and demands of her family and, second, a basic resourcefulness that permits her to make accommodations and at the same time to attain personal satisfaction. Her husband's mobility need not be detrimental to a woman's work if she is prepared to experiment with available opportunities. Withdrawal from work need not be traumatic if a woman finds deep satisfaction and stimulation from her role as wife, mother, and volunteer.

In actually working out the several adjustments and accommodations which life demands of her, a working woman may devote a part of her resourcefulness to persuading members of her family to take over some of the household duties and thus reduce the claims that they make on her. The success of different women depends in considerable measure on the personality of their husbands. Those who are flexible and sensitive to the needs of their wives can be as helpful as others are difficult. A husband who seeks employment in localities that will also provide his wife with career opportunities demonstrates as much adaptability as does a wife who modifies her goals in response to the requirements of her husband's job. So, too, does a man who agrees to limit the size of his family in order to facilitate his wife's career. On the other hand, a husband who is reluctant to assume any responsibilities about the home may limit his wife's opportunity to seek other sources of gratification.

Whatever the circumstances in which these women find themselves, they are one and all engaged in seeking that combination which will provide the greatest satisfaction. There is, of course, no single way of doing this. The best accommodation for one woman might not be tolerable for another. Moreover, no woman can assume that a resolution which is satisfactory at the moment will remain so. After all, they know that people change and circumstances change. Adapters understand more or less intuitively that their whole lives are characterized by continuing change, which requires continuing adjustment.

The Unsettled

The women who are classified as members of the group we have called the unsettled originally belonged to the planners, the recasters, or the adapters. But somewhere along the way their patterns of life have become clouded, and the steps which they were taking to fulfill their goals have faltered. They are uncertain and dissatisfied because their original plans have gone awry and because they have not yet found satisfactory ways of rearranging their lives.

A woman's expectations and plans are rarely fulfilled in every respect. Sometimes it is in one's aspiration concerning the world of work that one is disappointed; sometimes it is in an aspect of interpersonal relations. But most people, especially those who have had the opportunity to pursue higher education and to make decisions slowly, are able to design approaches that they can follow more or less satisfactorily. Some may have to make radical shifts to realize their goals, some may have to lower their expectations; but they are still able to find acceptable ways of life. This is not true of the unsettled. Here we find women who have encountered barriers along the way and have not yet found new paths to their goals, or new goals.

Thus the unsettled represent a group apart. Unlike the women in the other three groups, each of whom has found a *modus vivendi*, the unsettled are still in the throes of searching, of trying to fit themselves into the larger world. Some have

suffered a great deal of disappointment, and they know that
they can look forward to contentment only if they can find
better solutions to important problems in their lives.

These women so far have not been able to resolve satisfactorily their conflicting goals and circumstances. This is not to
say that they did not develop life goals. Most of them did, but
they have found part or all of them unsatisfactory or impossible to realize and they have been unable to develop more gratifying alternatives. Their dissatisfaction centers either about
their careers, or their personal lives, or both.

We will present self-portraits of three types of unsettled
women. The first two consist of women whose problems are
restricted either to the area of work or to personal lives. That
is to say, concerns in one of these areas have not significantly
affected other areas of their lives. The third type has problems
that were precipitated by difficulties either in their careers or
in their personal lives, but these have affected the totality of
their lives.

UNRESOLVED CAREER

Women who have spent at least 17 years in formal study are
understandably interested in making constructive use of their
education, more likely than not in paid work. Despite the long
preparation of our group, however, there were some who have
been thwarted in achieving their career goals. A few women
were close to acquiring their degrees when marriage or the necessity to earn a livelihood deflected them. When they left the
university, they found that their career goals could not be realized. For this group, failure to complete their education has
proved to be a serious roadblock.

Another group that is caught up in unresolved career problems is composed of women who regret that, because of personal or market considerations, they have been unable to make full use of their education and skills. Either family commitments have forced them to withdraw from work or they have had to take jobs which do not utilize their competence, or they have encountered one or another type of discrimination in the market place which has had the same result.

Others run into career troubles on more subtle grounds. A few women who made very large investments in preparing for and pursuing particular careers have developed, somewhere along the line, serious doubts about their chosen fields. But because of their heavy investments, they are loath to shift directions. They do not derive adequate satisfactions from their chosen fields but they are not yet able to forsake them and to seek more satisfying outlets. They are still the prisoners of their first choices.

Still others discover that having children has had unforeseen effects upon their careers. Some have had so many children, or their children are still so young, that they have not been able to free any significant portion of their time and energy for the pursuit of their careers, regardless of their desire to return to work.

All of these women, and others with different sources of dissatisfaction with their work, attach importance to careers. They are not exclusively concerned with their traditional roles as wives and mothers, with which they may be satisfied. Satisfaction with homemaking is not a sufficient criterion of success for them; these women find that gratification outside the home is also a necessary ingredient of their lives, and it is this that they find lacking.

Claire Lambert

My parents were anxious that I have a college education, and both worked to that end. My father did not care especially about what I did with my education, as long as I led a satisfied and happy life. My mother saw my intellectual competence, my academic honors, as a spear with which to shaft other women whose daughters were less bright and less well-educated. I was always a means to her ends, not a person in myself.

My father lost an electrical company in the 1929 stock market crash, drifted to New York from Louisiana, where I had been born in 1927, did odd jobs in the NRA, WPA, and FHA until 1936, when he landed a job as a salesman for a large chemical firm and we moved to St. Louis. He had had one year of college and my mother was a college graduate who had left elementary school teaching when she married. After my father's death in 1948, she went to work as a librarian and remained in the field for the following twelve years.

My father was a Roosevelt New Dealer, ebullient, loud, mercurial, and weak. My mother is conservative, prudish, unimaginative, cruel and cutting, strong and dominating. We have never gotten along. We never will. My parents' marriage was a violent and unhappy one. As a child I read to escape. Very early in life I became interested in Oriental civilizations, for what reason I cannot honestly say. When I entered college in 1944, I thought I would take one course in Chinese for the hell of it—I loved it and stayed on.

We moved around a lot during my youth and I went to high school in three different localities, finally graduating from one in Stamford, Connecticut. I then entered Smith, where I majored in foreign area studies, with special emphasis on the history and civilization of China. My major field encompassed history, philosophy, languages, and the economics of western Europe, the United States, the Middle East, and Latin America. With the exception of mathematics and music I took courses in almost every department at college. I was graduated magna cum laude in 1948, a member of Phi Beta Kappa, and a recipient of a fellowship for graduate study. I worked each summer during college, as a waitress, as a clerk, as a coat model, and as a companion to an elderly woman who did not like my cooking, my politics, or me.

My first and only career goal was to do diplomatic work in the Far East. When I was in college I believed (an opinion later confirmed by almost five years' residence and travel there) that world power is shifting back toward the Orient, specifically to China. The United States government needs personnel educated and keyed to the cultures of the Pacific. I attended graduate school to learn more in my field and to further my chances for employment in that area. My education in Chinese language and history at Columbia from first to last was magnificent—its excellence helped me to obtain and lose more than one good job.

I became a State Department employee after completing course credits for a M.A. in 1949, and I obtained the degree in 1950. Departmental requirements stipulated some experience in the Far East before continuing for the Ph.D. But I chose the diplomatic field at the wrong time in history. It was a deep disappointment to see people older and of greater education floundering, beaten, and broken, under a political persecution (McCarthy, Cohn, and Schine) no different from that experienced elsewhere in the world under dictatorships. Can you imagine the effect on me as a 22-year-old girl of seeing a great teacher and good friend reduced professionally and personally to ashes on charges known to me to be outright lies! I defended this teacher personally before a State Department panel; this, together with my advocacy of recognition of the Communist government in China, resulted in my being allowed to resign from the State Department's hot house atmosphere after 6 tumultuous weeks. I have never regretted the separation!

I then undertook work in the documentary division of a foreign military mission (NATO) and embassy which entailed providing information to the U.S. government for aid and personnel exchange purposes. Two years later I became an English language teacher at a Far Eastern university. I taught courses at the university level and to trainees at the National Police Academy. This was my finest work experience. I also taught English 6 hours a week in a local Chinese school system which was heavily financed by the "red" government in China. During the 2 years I worked there I was permitted to teach what I wished as I wished. No suggestions were made as to my personal or ideological behavior. The Chinese embassy officials were aware of the anomalous position I enjoyed as an American national and went out of their way to provide me with the materials and books I needed, to respond to each request courteously and quickly. My relations with my Chinese pupils and their parents were far superior to those with my other Asian students.

I also volunteered to be a group leader for thirty-five orphans who lived at a Buddhist temple and nunnery. I took them to festivals, picnics, outings, and such diverse and gaudy entertainment as the Chinese community provides these little ragamuffins. I enjoyed the color, confusion, and general bombast with which the old nuns did everything. In the process, I met and came to know Asians of every social stripe and political conviction, learning to work with them in the context of their civilization (and often to see the world as they saw it, which was frightening for a white woman when you consider what they really think of the white man at the very core of their being; and sad—because we deserve it).

On the other hand, my duties involved long hours of work and unsanitary conditions. Once, for 4 months, I lacked books, pencils, and paper; slept on a roach-infested mat (I got to like the roaches except when they crawled into my hair); had no medical facilities; and hence got malaria, dengue fever and round-worm. Yet, I would go back to it tomorrow. I like the Orient, and I loved teaching the little ones; physical discomfort cannot dispel the satisfaction of seeing the human mind open and flower.

I applied for the teaching job in Asia by writing to the dean of the faculty of letters at the local university. He was also co-ordinator and secretary of a division of the country's Communist Party (made known to me six weeks after my arrival). For almost 3 years, I handled his English language correspondence, professional, personal, and political. It was a rare and valuable insight into the "Communist" mind. The Communist Party, which was for many citizens their last hope, became a last chance for many Europeans and Americans as well. I cannot remember the number of missionaries, businessmen, students, tourists and drifters who made their way to the university and party headquarters for help. These were people whom the official diplomatic community either would not or could not help. The Communist Party paid transportation expenses, clothed, housed, fed these hardship cases, and got them out of the country. I handled the processing for most of these people, the majority of whom were Americans (I still receive Christmas cards from a few of them—after 10 years). For no extra salary and with Communist money and passes I did what American officials were highly paid to do, but did not. It was a very cold war in a very hot country.

When I returned to the United States in 1956, at the end of

my contract, I became an executive trainee and then an assistant buyer at a department store in Los Angeles because I could
not find employment in my field. I left after a year to get married and, the following year, became a researcher and writer
with a state educational association. I left 6 months later just
before my son was born and stayed at home with him for the
first 9 months. Since 1960 I have been employed as a market
researcher for an advertising firm. It bores me to death, but we
need the money ($100 a week) since my husband failed in
business the year I began. All my changes in jobs and in intellec-
ual and social pursuits have been dictated by financial pressures.
Many do not reflect my basic interests.

I spend 40 hours a week at work, many hours assisting in my
husband's work, and every other waking hour in housework,
reading, child-rearing, and theater and opera attending. My
husband is an antique dealer with some college credits and ar-
chitectural training. He is an absolutely kind, sensitive person.
His business difficulties since 1960 have been greatly aggra-
vated by his awareness that I am not doing what I would like
to be doing, by his struggle to provide a good and above-
average standard of living, and by my mother's constantly re-
minding him that he is a bum and a bastard because he failed in
business. Last year he developed severe angina pectoris because
of these continued pressures.

My mother is considerably embittered now that I have not
set the world on fire and has transferred her ambitions to my
son, who must succeed where I have failed. His health and
education are very important to my husband and me. We have
put him in the kindergarten of a French–English (bilingual)
school here where he is doing very well, and, barring death or
other misfortune, we will keep him in this school. I have a
maid who comes in one day a week, who is neither expensive
nor satisfactory, leaving me with the really heavy physical
household work to do. My husband and I have been able to

pay off the large debts which could not be taken into his bankruptcy, accumulate two pieces of property, including the
house we live in, place our son in a private school, and keep
sunny-side-up financially by extremely hard work.

I enjoy cooking—and being with my child. I really did
enjoy the months I was home with him. I shall always feel a
personal loss at not having been home with him during his preschool years. I dislike plain, old-fashioned household cleaning,
dusting, and the like. I am a meticulous housekeeper and resent
the psychological compulsion to keep things clean and tidy at
the expense of intellectual and educational pursuits. I have a
child, a husband, and a home, and they cannot be neglected.
My situation is not unique; to me it is the single greatest problem faced by the educated woman (and the woman longing
for more education).

At present, my only volunteer activity involves membership
in a symphony society. I support it financially and go to soi-
rees to shake the conductor's hand. The drinks are great, music
marvelous, and people terrible, but it's a break from home and
office despite being pure dribble and social climbing. I do a
great deal of reading of newspapers and periodicals in the
course of my work, but I am now years behind on books.
Reading gives me the entrée to foreign lands, art, politics, the
whole changing world which I would not otherwise have.
When I am too tired to read as much as I would like, I am just
that much less informed, that much farther behind. It is not
enough to age, we must also grow!

I had no formal education after obtaining my master's degree. I did have to learn an Asian language well enough to
teach in it at an elementary level. This was done in a haphazard
manner, largely a personal undertaking with little outside help.
My education has greatly conditioned my political, religious,
and cultural life, but it would be difficult for me to say where
the formal education ended and the practical one began. I am

as interested today in Far Eastern affairs as I was 13 years ago. Like it or not, the United States is being drawn square around to face the reality of China as a world power. Sinology as a field of study will regain its luster—if only by sheer necessity! It is still my hope to reenter this field, to get a Ph.D., and to do something with my education for my own people. When my husband's business activities are such that I can leave my job and go back to school, I will have to rebegin my education with a thorough review of the Chinese language, emphasizing the spoken, before I can go on for a doctorate in this field.

My education constituted an open door to many jobs and experiences as long as I was in the Orient. The reason for this is that the lack of educated personnel makes those who are educated of premium value. Sex never seemed to be a deterrent to my getting what I wanted from the Orientals or the Europeans. In America, my experience with prospective employers involves their giving my lengthy job experience a cursory glance, then anxiously asking, "But can you type?"

I would like to propose an educational program for women like myself, who need to earn a livelihood but desire more education. My proposal is, namely, that the U.S. government (or some private group if such there be) subsidize the student through his or her advanced education, allowing him enough money to support his family and live decently—a G.I. bill for civilians and especially for women. In return, the student must work for the government or the private group concerned for a certain number of years. This is hardly a novel idea and its cost would be but a fraction of the millions spent yearly on shoring up dictatorships throughout the world.

My comments on the American attitude toward the educated woman echo those of many educated women. There is a lack of interest in the kind, quality, and extent of a woman's education when it is unrelated to commercial skills. Women are automatically barred from *consideration* for executive positions because they are women. They are paid *very* much less than men for identically the same job. They are hired last and fired first. They are expected to have more and better qualifications for jobs men may fill with fewer and inferior credentials. They are subject to moral criticism and even dismissal for behavior which, in a man, would be dismissed with a simple "boys will be boys" attitude.

Intellectual ability, professional skills, and ambition in women are treated with envy, distrust, scorn, and outright hatred by many men. These attitudes are breaking down, but it will be a long time before we utilize the training of women to the extent that our Communist adversaries do. In the United States, women's talents are too often wasted, neglected, and denigrated. We are engaged in a struggle for world domination with an intelligent, organized, and determined antagonist. He may be doing poorly on the farm, but he is doing better than well in the classroom. He is using women's skills to the hilt. If, as some predict, this war will be won in the classroom, then, in respect to the utilization of the educated women, he has already taken a giant step toward victory.

Helen Irving

I was born in Shaker Heights, Ohio, in 1925, the daughter of native-born parents, both of whom were high school graduates. My father lost a printing business in the early 1930's and was a salesman thereafter, with many different jobs, basically selling things which were mostly gadgets of one sort or another. His printing business had been successful, but after losing that, he never was successful financially. I grew up in the Depression and came from a home with significant problems, both economic and emotional. My mother had several nervous breakdowns—recurrent depressions. Her only work experi-

ence was as a saleswoman for a brief period while I was in high
school, a job she took because of financial need. She divorced
my father when I was 12 and remarried "for financial security" 2 years later.

Both my parents were interested in "cultural things," i.e.,
piano lessons even if we didn't eat, but with the limited educational backgrounds of my parents, our house was not intellectually stimulating, or emotionally or economically secure. I
just didn't know who I was and somehow couldn't seem to
talk any of my problems out. In addition, we were Jewish, and
I felt that this was an added burden. When I finished high
school I actually got my father to legally change our name to
one that sounded less Semitic.

I think I did not have major emotional difficulties because I
got satisfaction from doing well in school, from getting A's. I
did not develop real interests in one subject or another; I just
had to do well in everything. Also, I was able to make a few
good friends, which made a difference in managing to get
along. There were signs of emotional difficulty along the way,
but each was self-limited, and I seemed able to pull myself
back on the academic-A treadmill.

My mother deprecated homemaking. She was frustrated in
her own vocational goals and quite bitter about her lot. She
wanted everything for her children. My brother left home
when he was 21 and I was 11. He quit college after one year,
married, and got a job. My mother's goal for my brother was
medicine. I somehow, without awareness, took it over during
my early teens. I graduated from high school at 16, and the
events leading me into medicine all just happened very quickly
and irrevocably.

In 1941 I entered the University of Michigan, where I majored in chemistry and was graduated at the end of three years
since I was on an accelerated wartime program. This meant
spending summers at college and being swiftly carried along

through the selected program with very little flexibility. I funneled my time and energy into the subjects related to my "medical ambition" and career. At college I did do some modern dancing, which I loved, but rejected it because of its interference with my medical goal, and because of anxieties it stirred up, i.e., fear of losing control. Originally, my goal was to *become* a doctor; I did not anticipate the continuing practice of medicine. In addition to my mother's influence, I think I chose a medical career because I thought that in becoming a doctor I could be somebody, though of course it did *not* work out that way—I had the same insecurities upon completion of medical school as before. Neither honors, Phi Beta Kappa, Alpha Omega Alpha (a medical honor society), nor other tangible achievements seemed to make any difference. I did what I did well because I had to and not because I enjoyed the doing of it. Oh, I got some satisfaction out of it, but relatively little. Another reason I settled on becoming a doctor is more difficult to explain, but I think it is also valid. Somehow, certainly without awareness, I equated death to loss—and my sensitivity to loss has been very striking. Somewhere, somehow, I think I wanted in some magic way to prevent death and dying.

When I graduated from college in 1944, and just before entering medical school, I was married to a lawyer. My husband supported my educational endeavor. At several crucial times when I was discouraged and considered abandoning it, he was the single factor that gave me the kind of friendly positive assurance I needed to go on. In no way do I mean financial support, for I was on scholarship much of the time. I had a very unrealistic point of view about the problem of combining marriage and career. I just felt it would somehow, again magically, work out. To whatever extent it has now worked out had nothing to do with "magic!"

After I graduated from medical school in 1948, I served an internship at a Chicago hospital, followed by a residency in

dermatology at a hospital in a nearby suburb. By that time, I
had overt anxiety about making an error that would lead to a
patient's death, and this influenced my choice of dermatology
as a specialty.

Shortly after completing my residency in 1950, I gave birth
to my first son and stayed home for the next 4 years to care
for him and my second son, who was born in 1953. During
part of this period, I was active in politics as president of the
local Democratic club in the suburb where we lived. The politics helped to pull me out of the morass which I felt myself in
when I stayed home and had the children. I had kept to myself, got little pleasure out of my home, and had few outside
interests. I was asked to go into politics and just did it although
I had no real feeling for it before I got into it. I did have positive feelings about getting Eisenhower out of office and Ste-
venson in and, in addition, it was satisfying because it got me
into the world and into contact with all sorts of people. I
went out of my way to talk to many different kinds of people.
I did dislike the organizational-type busywork however. These
years at home were troubled years. Life-long problems were
accentuated and became pressing. I became depressed, seriously in 1955, and began psychoanalytic therapy.

In 1956, I returned to medicine, taking a part-time position
as a research assistant in dermatology at a medical school in
Chicago. This was a "safe" research project where I could
avoid the conflicts I had involving treatment of seriously ill patients. After 2 years, I was able to expand my hours to full-
time since my children were both in school. Then, for 6
months in 1960, I tried private general practice, working on a
20-hours-per-week schedule. I found private practice satisfying but also worrisome and *anxiety*-producing. I was overly
concerned with sick patients, and worried about incorrect
decisions. I feel in all that I practiced good medicine, but it
took a lot out of me and my family, although I admit that if I

wanted to I might be able to work this out. In any event, when I was called in suddenly to see my neighbor who died of a coronary (I did what I could, but to no avail) I went into a gradual but deep depression that lasted months and was resolved only as the cause became clear. It seems that the motivating factors in my selection of medicine were spurious; the fact that I have gotten some satisfaction out of it is unrelated to the need to be somebody and to prevent death. It stems from my ability to directly involve myself with medicine and people.

I received a Public Health Service grant in 1961 and returned to part-time research. The following year I received another grant, this time at the hospital where I had interned, and I am now working 16 hours a week at a yearly salary of $4,000. As a human being, I gained and continue to gain enormously from the experience and privileged relationships that go with doctoring, in the awareness of people as whole human beings which the study of medicine has fostered. I somehow feel I know more about people than I would have if I had studied something else. I enjoy contact with patients and other doctors, the interpersonal relationships.

However, I now know I turned away from or gave up things that have turned out, 15 to 20 years later, to be of great importance to me, to give me satisfaction, to feel very "right." In 1955 I became interested in and started painting; I went to school weekly for over 4 years. This became and is an active growing interest. I now spend from 10 to 14 hours a week painting and 8 to 10 hours as a discussion leader in a local college extension introductory course in art appreciation.

Although my painting is not a "job" in the accepted sense of salaried work, I regard it as major work. It is the hardest thing I've ever had the courage to try and stick to. The discipline has to be within (in distinction to being imposed from the outside). I'm involved in the struggle, and expect it will continue

for years. Even when I am deeply discouraged, when I finally
get at the easel there is a kind of satisfaction that's hard to describe, but is real, more real than many other so-called achievements I have known in the past. I have not resolved whether I
should or should not continue in medicine. I cannot seem to
give my present job the kind of dedicated service and commitment I think it deserves. I may finally choose to devote more
time to becoming a better painter if possible. I hope to continue to simplify my life where I can, to refuse extra jobs unless they are things I really want to do. I want more time for
painting one way or the other! Yet, the decision to focus away
from medicine and toward art has been difficult for me and it
is not fully accepted even now. Answering the present survey
added to the conflict; I think that is why it took me so long to
fill in the questionnaire. I've been working it out for at least a
year if not longer. But it is clear that my involvement and
commitment is limited, and that other areas in the arts are
much more meaningful. I have no question of the priority of
these things over science and medicine. When I had to do
something that was organized for me from the outside, medicine was "easier" than creative tasks. Until about 6 years ago
everything I did had to be under my rigid control; now I feel
freer to "fall apart" and "come together" again, and this makes
a tremendous difference.

I think that there is a particular problem for the child and
adolescent coming from deprived backgrounds (and this is
often coupled with a minority problem as well). The selection
of vocational goals by these youngsters is fraught with great
obstacles, and careful guidance and real rapport with "key"
adults is necessary so that "false" goals can be evaluated. Except for an art teacher in high school, my key persons did not
appear until much later in life. They were an artist with whom
I studied, both a remarkable teacher and a remarkable human
being, who influenced me greatly; and a psychoanalyst to

whom I went for over 6 years, who worked with me to allow me to resolve some of my incapacitating conflicts.

As far as my family life is concerned, our location is definitely guided by my husband's practice, which usually produces an annual income of between $15,000 and $20,000. He has many interests in addition to his work but they are *very* different from mine. My husband's attitude is difficult to get down in few words. He doesn't, in principle or in practice, object to my working. He does feel however, first, that I should always accept the household as my responsibility and, second, that I should not use my work situation to "run away" from him, from my children, or from our way of life.

Until 4 or 5 years ago I got *no* satisfaction from homemaking whatsoever. It was important for me to get out and work because I was too involved (and guilty) about my two boys. But once I worked my personal problems out, I geared my work schedule to my boys' needs within reason, always managing to get household help when I needed it. I have come to realize I don't want to work just to get out of the house. A job must have positive aspects in and of itself to be worthwhile. For the past few years I have been getting considerable satisfaction from making our home a reflection of what we are— our interests, our values, and so on. But I still hate having to fight the battle against clutter, the battle against the loss of style and taste in living; there is so much shoddiness everywhere. I dislike supermarket shopping and living and I go out of my way to avoid it.

Most of my leisure activities are pursued in the summer. Among them are boating, sailing, and some small amount of gardening (I'm a good weed puller but not particularly creative at it). I love the ocean, the shore, the slow pace of summer—time to walk along the beach, look, listen, do nothing. I spend more time over summer reading and painting. This is *a time to sort experiences.*

Today, I can finally value the positive qualities of both my parents. My father is a compassionate and kind human being. That he is a "failure" in economic things seems of little importance now. My mother, too, has grown in the last 10 years and is more a person in her own right.

My experience has taught me that careers for women are worthwhile if they represent positive and real goals, which give pleasure and satisfaction in the very doing of the activity selected. If this *is* the case I believe patterns of home life can be arranged. Compromises can be made at periods of peak load and goals kept in sight for a future time. On the other hand, if a career is used or is desired because one is running away from oneself, from something else, or for other spurious goals, then I think a career is inappropriate and "wrong." Further, those who run are the people (men and women) who have the difficulties, such as anxieties, depressions, and guilt. I have found that I can put up with many negative factors if I have to, *if* and only *if* there are definite positive satisfactions, enough of them, and at frequent enough intervals to look forward to!

I think the value of higher education for women is unquestionable. It opens doors to a way or ways of living that are valuable irrespective of whether the woman follows a career part-time, full-time, or not at all. I believe people should be involved in meaningful activities throughout their lives, and that how one accomplishes this (in reference to such things as family and child bearing) can be worked out and will vary from person to person. The very fact that much of the time women don't have to support families gives them greater freedom to follow those avenues that basically and integrally interest them.

As of now, I plan to stop working some time next spring and to devote my full time for a year or two (at least) to painting. When and if I want to return to work, I don't know whether I shall seek some area in medicine. I feel I may want to try and work in some capacity in a university setup, working with college people and closer to areas to which I am committed. I know I have thoroughly enjoyed being a discussion leader in the art appreciation course now that I have gotten over my initial (and usual) anxiety over something new.

Barbara Newman

My Polish immigrant parents had no formal education, but they always felt that their three daughters should continue their education as far as possible. My sisters and I grew up in the Depression and yet, as each of us was graduated from high school, there was never a doubt in my parents' minds that we should go to college. My father, who worked for a wholesale butcher in Brooklyn, couldn't manage a tuition college, but we all did very well at Hunter, a public college. We all worked part-time during our college years, but never more than a few hours a week, and earned enough for subway fare and small articles of clothing, such as stockings and sweaters. During the summers, we took courses, and my parents even then would allow us to work only a few hours a week so we'd have plenty of time for reading and studying. Their attitude has had a tremendous influence on me, in two ways: First, I do want to complete the Ph.D. finally and quickly and, second, I feel a great responsibility to my own children to do at least as much for them in their quest for an education as my parents have done for my sisters and me. They wanted their daughters to marry, and we all did, but my own desire to get married was not necessarily influenced by their attitude. And my parents are happy to have their daughters work, but I know they are terribly upset by any sign of neglect of their grandchildren.

When I was graduated from college in 1946 at the age of 21, I felt I was "unfinished." Since I was interested in teaching

humanities at the college level, graduate study followed as a
matter of course. I was also interested in physics and received
A's in my college courses, but it did not compare to my interest in my major field. I recall now that I never even thought of
not doing graduate work.

I received a grant for a year's study at Columbia, where I
received a master's degree in 1947. I then continued my graduate studies at another university with the intention of acquiring
a Ph.D. Two years later, I became a part-time teaching assistant there, which helped pay some expenses and gave me experience while I was a graduate student. In 1952, after completing my course requirements, I became an instructor and freshman advisor at a coeducational university in the East. That
year, I was married to a professor in the same department and,
although I continued to teach, after five years I was refused
promotion to an assistant professorship because of my husband's position in that department. I was offered a part-time
lectureship instead which I took because there was no alternative. This appointment was terminated after one year and I
then began to teach part-time at a nearby university where I
am still employed. It seemed like a good idea to leave the
campus where my future was not secure.

My 5 years of instructorship from 1952 to 1957 gave me my
best experience as a teacher, since I gave a great variety of
courses and had some administrative experience. However, I
spent much more time at this than I should have. I should have
completed the dissertation during *that* period in my life. Now
I have three young children and it's much more difficult to
steal the time.

My husband was divorced and still pays alimony to his first
wife, a factor which has had a decisive influence on my continuing to teach, even part-time, during these past years when
I probably should have completed the dissertation. I could

never manage the home, children, teach, and do my research with the limited household help we can afford when I do teach. Child support is easing up since the younger of my husband's two children by his former marriage is about to reach maturity. I would leave my present position if there were an opportunity to go to another college of at least equal rank for a better salary, a fuller program of teaching, and *most important* a teaching assignment with a wider variety of courses.

My children are close in age. I currently spend 5 hours each week teaching, about 15 hours working on my dissertation, and uncounted hours on homemaking. Before I was married, I felt unwilling to compromise on any aspect of either marriage or career. I wanted to complete my graduate study successfully, and wanted just as much to run a fine home, be a good wife, and have children. Now I find the necessity to care for the children and to run my home so that my husband can discharge his responsibilities with relative peace of mind is the most forceful influence on how I spend my time. Nothing takes precedence over these activities. I was amazed to find that as my children grew older, they seemed to need me more of the time. I sometimes help them with school work; I must transport them around town for music lessons, religious school; and so on. In other respects, of course, they're more independent. I guess a part-time position for me is easiest on them, although I think I'll be able to manage more this coming year when my youngest will have a full day in school. I find "puttering" around the house terribly boring and the daily chores real drudgery. Of course, the teaching schedule cannot be tampered with, but the introductory courses I teach require limited preparation mainly because I've had so much experience with them. As a matter of fact, in order to keep myself interested, I change the illustrative materials in the basic courses and that takes some time. Frankly, if I wanted to do it the *very* easiest way, I could really spend 10 minutes or so before each class and do a good job, too. That becomes a bit boring, though, and discourages growth on my part.

The one activity to which I turn after everything else gets done, but which is on my mind constantly, however, is working on my dissertation. The pressure there is of my own making—nobody is pushing me into it, but it's as real as though the deadline came from outside sources. My husband now holds important administrative posts and he seems to need me more. We go out together much more and entertain much more, both of which activities I love and need, but then there is the remorse I feel for all the time spent that could have been put in on the dissertation.

I love to teach and I find that one's relationships with one's students can be very exciting and stimulating. Also, I learn much more about my field when I teach than I do through studying alone. Like so many teachers, I dislike grading exams. Reading essays can be gratifying, but if there are too many and there is a real deadline, it becomes a chore. Furthermore, I'm convinced that just doing a really fine job isn't enough to insure success in the future. There are too many irrelevant considerations which are given lots of importance. I once considered changing to law, but I'm getting a little too old to begin going to law school. I *love* to teach my own subject; moreover we need the money that I can earn as a part-time lecturer.

My husband's position has been something of a hindrance to me professionally because we meet socially with most of those people whom I must contact when looking for a teaching position. It would seem that this situation might be helpful, but it isn't. I cannot make myself inquire about a position from people who have come to know me either as their hostess or more specifically as my husband's wife. I find it embarrassing to ask for a job. I was amazed and crushed when told confidentially

by a ranking professor in another local college that his department had consulted with the president of the college about the
advisability of hiring the wife of a man in my husband's position as a one-year replacement for someone in the department.
The president's attitude was that it was all right—as a one-year
replacement.

My studies govern almost all my activities outside of those
under the specific heading of "homemaking." Of course, the
situation might have been different if I hadn't married someone also vitally interested in the same field. I really don't
know. But as I look at our social activities, I see that our
friends are mainly people of similar interests—we entertain
them and they invite us to their homes. We attend meetings of
learned societies and programs related to our work. Organiz-
ing activities for the children so they might profit from my
professional training is very important to me as well as time-
consuming. I am also a well-prepared sounding board for my
husband's ideas when he's writing an article or a book.

I've been disappointed and discouraged since leaving school
much more than I ever anticipated during my school years.
Prizes and honors I've received look fine on a *curriculum vitae*,
but I'm not sure that after all is said and done, they make too
much difference. I'm 38 years old now and still have not been
able to capture a real appointment, with rank and salary, although I honestly think I'm a very good teacher. Good teaching
doesn't seem to get enough consideration from administrators
on the college level. Moreover, I've begun to publish articles
and reviews rather steadily now. I have been reviewing manu-
scripts for publishers and advising them, criticizing content, and
the like. This helps me to know firsthand what kind of
material is being considered for publication. This much experience in any other field would have brought me much
more attractive salaries (I earn about $2,500 a year) and ad-
vantages.

If I had completed my doctorate, however, I don't think I would have met with too much disappointment. However, I am aware that most departments feel that they're safer with a man, and they are, since a married woman has the pressing responsibility of caring for her husband or children in case of illness, for example. If a professional woman can have full-time responsible help at home, even illness shouldn't be too much of a problem. Also, I've noticed that it is assumed that a man may take his work more seriously, since he must actually support himself and possibly a family, too.

It is not easy for a woman to have a husband and children as well as a career, but it can be done, and for some women (I'm thinking of myself) it is an absolute necessity. Women have demonstrated that they can achieve as high a degree of excellence in their fields as men, and careers for women must follow automatically. Married women must do justice to their families as well as their careers, but if they can work out their problematic dual existence, they should not be hampered in their efforts. I feel convinced that any difficulty I have now in finding a position (I don't mean part-time teaching, but a tenure-bearing appointment) will virtually disappear when I complete the Ph.D. degree. Perhaps I will not have as broad a choice as a man with the equivalent of my educational background and teaching experience, but I anticipate much easier sailing in my career.

PERSONAL DISCONTENT

Some women come to realize that their lives are not yielding them much personal satisfaction. Some of these women are single. Many had opportunities to marry but passed them up. Others had been loath to trade their educational goals or their careers for the uncertain joys of marriage. Later these women realize that their careers are not enough. They want and need close ties to others. But for many of them, realization comes late, although most of them believe that some day they may have the chance to marry. Although they achieve success and satisfaction in their careers, they feel that their lives are incomplete, without close personal ties.

There are other women who marry, but who later find that their marriages do not provide the satisfactions they had anticipated. Often, such marriages end in divorce and the women then seek new marital relationships. These women feel that marriage and families are necessary components of a good life. While trying to resolve their personal problems many of them engage in gratifying work. But this is not enough. It is simply a way of marking time until they remarry. Whether they will later continue to work is problematical. For them, it is important to achieve fulfillment in the non-work area of their lives.

Widows frequently have an approach similar to that of divorcees. Many of them also are unhappy because of the void in their personal lives. Whether they remain at home or whether they work, they are unable to come to terms with their widowhood, and they seek new mates.

Rebecca Etienne

I was brought up in South Hadley, Massachusetts, where my father was a professor of history at Mount Holyoke College. My mother was a college graduate who was employed as a bookkeeper before her marriage. She undertook no regular employment after she married, but assisted my father in his research. She also wrote articles for publications and painted for sale and for personal pleasure. Thus, she derived gratification in matching the family scale of intellectual offerings. I have a

younger sister who is married to a professor and has two children. She has her M.A. and teaches Spanish in high school and
college.

College was inevitable but it had to be at home. Job choices,
travel, friends, and so on flowed quite predictably from the
college environment in which we grew up. Among the major
influences on my life I include the following: Dickens, who
brought dreams of other lives, other problems; "colorful" and
stimulating teachers whose enthusiasm for discussion and
strong points of view challenged me to keep on my toes intellectually, take positions, and enjoy debate; piano lessons and
piano teachers who made strong impressions by opening a variety of musical doors; and dance teachers and performance
opportunities which gave me the desire to transmit this pleasurable vehicle to others.

I entered Mount Holyoke in 1943, when I was 17. My goal
was a college degree and marriage. I originally planned to
major in English literature, but I shifted to government in my
junior year for the sake of an available appointment as an exchange student at McGill. Thereafter, the marketability of
government as a field relegated the field of my greater interest
to a hobby. I had a full-tuition scholarship throughout college,
and I worked as a camp counselor in the summers and as an
usher at concerts during the year. By graduation, marriage had
become my primary goal and continued to be so.

After receiving my B.A. in 1947, I was selected as an intern
at the National Institute of Public Affairs. I was assigned to
serve as a hearings reporter, and I also worked at the Library
of Congress and at the State Department. I took a statistics
course at George Washington University at night. Following
my internship, I received a full-tuition scholarship award from
Columbia toward a master's degree in the Department of Public Law and Government. (Government had been my college
major and not only was I interested in it, but I anticipated

probable success in Federal Government employment. There appeared to be less marketability for my interest in literature or art.) My motives for undertaking graduate study were a combination of the possibility of professional advancement, the need for new horizons, new professors, social contacts, and intellectual curiosity. It seemed a logical flow and the best of alternative ways of spending my time.

For the summer following my year of courses toward the M.A., I became a tutor of English to a family in Belgium. This fulfilled a desire to travel, to perfect my French, and to get material for my thesis, which concerned that country. I later performed research and analysis for a professor at the University of Brussels which utilized my recent research and education.

In 1951, my thesis uncompleted, I returned to the United States when my money ran out and became a research fellow for the State Department. I received a fellowship to complete my thesis and returned to Belgium to do so the following year. In 1953, I came home to be married, having completed my work and having received my M.A. My husband was a graduate student and teaching fellow at Columbia. I had not visualized myself as continuing to pursue further graduate work as a permanent combination with housewifery, unless and until children had left the fold. Thus, any conflict I may have had between family and a career was resolved in the direction of "woman's place is in the home" and the desire to utilize my graduate training as stimulation for the kind of man I would marry and home I would like to keep.

However, I had to work until my husband's degree was completed and this deferred my having children. I took the most stimulating job available in the New York area, which was as a research director and press officer for a planning association. I left this job to work for a political organization, since it meant advancement and I needed the money that this job paid. During this period I began to feel that I was in a rut, and I started taking courses in municipal administration at NYU to explore a possible alternative career development. However, after 2 years I found that continuing in my former field was the course of least resistance and had the greatest financial and interest opportunities and the least frustrations. Also, municipal administration began to appear as an intensely frustrating career, as decisions foundered in political obstinacies.

I was divorced in 1958 and had to rely on my own career development again for income and opportunity to spend, travel, or buy a home. I left New York for Washington where I have been working since at various positions with the Federal Government. I am now engaged in research and operations work in international affairs at a salary of $9,000. I could have had an overseas assignment with the government, but personally I seemed to find greater pleasure in staying at home. I was reluctant to foray into new friendships in a doubtful social milieu when I had a very full and social life in Washington, with constant new friendships. I am not a suffragette and I am unwilling to put in the extra devotion to career or job which might entitle me to further advances.

In addition to my full-time job, I spend about one hour a month in minor writing, 4 hours a week as a student of painting and music, and an additional few hours at social gatherings and renovating my house. Dallying in art and music and redoing my house dominates my conversational offerings at the expense of job-derived topics. They give me pleasure and fill my time with something worthwhile. I love to make things (in the garden, the kitchen, the house at large). It is a change of pace from my job and the usual social frippery, and I get gratifications from "something to show" for effort.

In the past, I was a volunteer dance teacher for the mentally ill and for slum children, and I received a great deal of satisfaction from their response and from the improvement in my skills and my sense of achievement. There is much less satisfaction in adult civic activities, where idle housewives slightly improve their dilettante skills at your expense, and none from meetings for the sake of meetings, even if supposedly stimulating topics are tossed around, if they seem to lead to no beneficial action. And I'd rather have someone else take care of such tedia as alumnae activities, red feather fund raising, and the like.

On my job, I like seeing a project through to completion, the feeling of essentiality of the job completed. I am pleased when I satisfy someone who feels my work is either good or worthwhile and when I successfully supervise staff members and give them the satisfaction of knowing they've done a job well. It is also good to have the "right" position prevail in negotiation with other governments or departments. There are some routine chores I dislike, and I don't relish having to complete assignments that I consider meaningless. I would change my field if home life demanded moving to another location or if an opportunity arose for a worthwhile job in a demanding area which could utilize my skills while I was learning. If I remarried, the interests of a husband would distinctly affect my choices of activities and jobs.

Professionally, my career choice has been successful. In terms of personality, I imagine I would prefer to be steeped in the arts and things of this sort rather than a success in the competitive arena of Federal Government and political science scholarship, and that I would be happier personally if the alternative course had been followed.

My father has consistently urged more graduate training and the possibility of college teaching as a career. My scattered approach to the many competing uses of time has finally made him give up. Mother is more gratified than he by my salary. She has high ambitions for me: "Foreign service posts are influential," and so on. Her feeling that marriage can be too humdrum and careers are more interesting I resisted within the limits of the possibilities before me. My father is more concerned that I am not doing what I most want—raising children. Both feel professional persons are more interesting and have the only rewarding lives, and I agree, I fear.

Women who are married, with children, and who also want to work should do so, provided their homes do not suffer. But this means including time for leisure with husband and children, orderliness of housekeeping, stability of atmosphere for the children, and being sure that the wife's interest is not scattered too far for real fulfillment. (This can be done, even in the face of a husband's hostility to a career wife, if done adroitly.) On the other hand, those who don't want to follow this course should not be pushed; they should work only to achieve enough satisfactions, passively or by participation, to maintain the level of intellectual alertness and offering they desire.

PERSONAL AND CAREER DISSATISFACTION

A few women do not find satisfaction either in their work or in their interpersonal relations. General dissatisfaction is not a widespread phenomenon; it is characteristic of but a small proportion of the highly educated women in our study.

The key to the dissatisfaction of most of these women lies in the wide gap between what they expected and what has in fact turned out to be the facts of their lives. It would not be correct to say that their expectations have been excessive and that a sense of failure stems from inordinate anticipations. On the contrary—they hoped to find satisfaction in their work, and they looked forward to successful marriages. But somehow or other these simple objectives have remained unfulfilled. They feel frustrated in their work and they are unhappy in their personal lives.

The shortcomings they have found in their work are reflected primarily by a discrepancy between their potentialities and skills and the relatively modest progress that they have been able to make. Some hold jobs that do not utilize their education and training sufficiently; for a few, the matter is not sufficient utilization but inadequate recognition and rewards. Others miss the work they gave up in favor of homemaking.

On the personal side, some women, who remained single, feel with each passing year more unhappy and frustrated; some wives have husbands who are insensitive or unsympathetic to their needs and desires; others are unable to establish any rapport with their mates.

In many of these cases, problems in one sphere of life give rise to equally pressing problems in others. For example, marital difficulties precipitate career anxieties, or the reverse occurs. We know that concern with one aspect of life is usually reflected at least to some degree elsewhere. For these women, however, dissatisfaction that often had a single origin has become widely diffused.

Muriel Cramer

My home town, in northern Wisconsin, is the site of a small family-owned corporation of which my father has been president since 1950. He entered the business after graduation from college, working for my grandfather under a very paternalistic system. He married a high school graduate from a small town in Indiana and they had two children. I was born in 1927 and my sister was born 6 years later. She has a Master of Fine Arts degree, and is now a housewife and part-time student working toward teaching certification.

During my high school years, my mother began to work in the family business to obtain additional funds for my college education. Recently, my father has had several extended periods of illness, and because of his poor health my mother presently bears the major responsibility for running the firm. My parents' occupational experience gave me a strong desire for geographical mobility. I felt that my father, who has an alert, speculative mind and interest in literature, had missed opportunities by returning to the family business after college.

My parents encouraged me to combine work and marriage and felt that there need be no conflict between these goals. Education was considered highly important in a family where both paternal grandparents had some college or normal school training, and I was encouraged to set high goals.

In 1945 I entered Grinnell College. My goals during my early college years ranged from advertising to medicine to zoology. I soon abandoned the first of these aims, then gave up the idea of medicine because it seemed financially impossible to plan on 3 or 4 additional years in medical school. My family discouraged a zoology major because they considered my poor eyesight a handicap in microscopic work. I now know this was excessive precaution and that my eyesight would not have been a problem, but under the influence of my father, a college English major, I was directed toward literature and the humanities, finally choosing romance languages as a major.

With regard to a career, I feel that there was almost too much family influence directing me toward the humanities. However, I also came from a small high school with a weak science program. My tentative interest in science was not encouraged and I was steered into the humanities before I had any real chance to sample the sciences. In college, I was the sort of student who got A's in everything and found all areas of study interesting. Perhaps it is only wishful thinking to talk of other paths I might have followed and I may only be protesting against specialization in any field, but I feel that the student who might follow many successful routes does need very careful counseling. At times, I think that if I were in biological chemistry as a vocation and had the humanities as an avocation, I would be really enthusiastic about my field. As it is, I am moderately content, but unable to feel that much of what we do has any great significance for mankind.

I was elected to Phi Beta Kappa in my junior year, and graduated summa cum laude in 1949. By the time of graduation, having been strongly encouraged by my professors, I had decided to enter college teaching. Therefore, I applied for and received a scholarship from Columbia to pursue graduate studies in French. I received an A.M. after a year of study and became an instructor at a Midwestern college that year. During my 2 years of teaching I became aware that I needed more training if I were to be serious about my career. Since I also knew that the school was about to reduce its staff by 10 percent, I decided to resume graduate studies in order to qualify for a Ph.D. Therefore, in 1952, I entered the University of Minnesota, where I remained for 5 years as a graduate fellow. During this time, my parents amply supplemented my fellowships. In 1957, I was a Fulbright fellow in France, but returned home the following year to recuperate from hepatitis which I had contracted abroad. During my convalescence I worked on my dissertation. After a year at home, I applied for a teaching appointment and accepted the best of the offers as an instructor at a small coeducational college at a starting salary of $5,700, (for a 15-hour teaching load). There was definite prejudice against women in the major universities at that time. This is diminishing, largely because of a shortage of qualified men in romance languages and related fields, but it still affects the rate of promotion. I planned to remain there until I received my doctorate and then to join a university faculty, but I developed such an intense dislike of life at a small college that

I considered leaving teaching and perhaps going into the family business or some field which could use language preparation. Fortunately, I received a job offer 2 years later from a state university which I accepted because I knew that a position as an instructor there meant professional advancement plus a university atmosphere with the cultural facilities, library, and colleagues actively interested in research that are almost essential to my existence. This was a most crucial point in my career and has made a very great difference. In fact, I cannot state emphatically enough the overall effect of at last having the kind of position I trained for. I finally received my Ph.D. in 1963, but there is no question that full-time employment as a college instructor while writing my thesis seriously delayed its completion.

This year I switched to an instructorship at another state university where I earn $7,000, and my abrupt change of jobs was for a reason that would never affect a man's teaching career. During the previous Christmas vacation I became engaged to a student who had recently finished his Ph.D. Since we planned to be married in June and he was teaching in another state, I resigned to join him in the fall. Several months after the engagement was announced and after my replacement had been hired, my fiancé suffered a near nervous breakdown. I then learned that he had previously been under psychiatric treatment for several years. In view of the relapse, his doctor said that marriage at any time was out of the question. My present job was the best opportunity at a very late date in the academic hiring year.

I have suffered in terms of promotion, since at the time I resigned a departmental recommendation for promotion had been sent to the administration and in all probability would have been granted. Unfortunately, since I was jobless when the new opening occurred, I had no bargaining power. In the long run, the change may turn out to be a very desirable one, but it is hard to be convinced at the moment. If I had not re-signed, I would have been teaching a graduate course this year, and here I am, in a sense, starting all over again.

Outside of my work, I have spent a few hours a month on activities connected with affairs of the American Association of University Professors (AAUP). I also have been active in the past in the American Association of University Women (AAUW), whose program, particularly on the national level, is highly valuable. My primary leisure activities are reading and "creative" cooking. I read quite widely in fields not strictly my speciality. Cooking is one of the few "manual" tasks I am good at. It also represents a complete shift from my daily work.

As far as my career itself is concerned, I find my choice of field only relatively satisfactory. I do not feel the satisfaction I should in being a teacher, although I enjoy my work on a day-to-day basis. I highly respect the professor under whom I did my thesis. His type of scholarship and teaching provides a model when I get disillusioned about much of what passes for criticism and teaching. But I have less respect for the academic profession than I had 10 years ago. There is much less time for research and continuing education in my field than I previously expected to have, although my new job promises a much improved balance between teaching and research obligations. My greatest gratification comes from research and from working with the student who becomes intensely interested in literature and how it is put together.

I still hope to combine marriage with a career. I always naively assumed they could be combined without difficulty. However, this is probably the major unresolved problem in my life. A career by itself is not enough.

Evelyn Davidson

Both of my parents were from farming communities in Kansas and I, too, was born and raised in a rural area of that state. My father was a farmer and served as county agricultural commissioner for 12 years. He completed one year of college, but my mother did not go beyond grade school. Prior to her marriage, she had been employed as a maid and governess in Denver for 2 years, since she wished to travel and broaden her experience. She never engaged in paid employment thereafter.

I was the third in a family of four children. My older sister is now a homemaker and both of my brothers are farmers. We were always encouraged to make the most of our abilities. Our parents had a very liberal attitude. They placed great faith in education and I was encouraged to take all the schooling I thought I needed. Sacrifices were made so I could go to college and graduate school. I went to school during the war years when, fortunately, farmers had a little more money than at other times. Otherwise, my education might have been quite a burden. My parents' occupation of farming was a negative incentive. I studied and worked hard in order to get away from the economic uncertainties of life on the farm.

In 1942, when I was 17, I entered Kansas Wesleyan University, where I took a liberal arts course with major emphasis on English and speech. I was elected to Phi Beta Kappa. So few men were on campus because of the war that I had opportunities for leadership (such as president of the student council and editor of the college paper) that I might not otherwise have had. For the same reason perhaps, I married late; I was 26. I also worked one summer as a reporter on a Kansas paper. After graduating, I found I had no skill that I could readily market. I had thought I might like to do newscasting, but they weren't hiring women in that field in those days. So I decided to do graduate work in journalism, since it promised to broaden my horizons and to provide an opportunity for leadership through the written word.

I applied to Columbia, guided by the advice of a college friend, who had preceded me there, and was admitted on the condition that I take 9 hours of government and history to supplement what I had taken at college. These courses in imperialism, world politics, and the Far East eventually affected my choice of career.

I received my M.S. in journalism in 1947 and was hired by the Carnegie Endowment for International Peace as an editor. This was an excellent opportunity for a beginning journalist and I worked there for 3 years, changing in 1950 to a research position with the United Nations Secretariat. My career as a journalist seemed to lead very logically to a career in the United Nations, from research to application of research. I was married that year to a staff member of the American delegation to the UN. My husband has an M.A. in International Affairs from Columbia.

I continued working for the UN in various research capacities for the next 6 years. My work gave me the feeling of having made the most of my educational opportunities and of contributing in some small way to the betterment of mankind. I also was gratified by the salary (I reached $6,500), the travel opportunities, and the daily associations with interesting people. My employers had one thing in common: They hired and promoted solely on the basis of ability, not sex. For them, the battle over women's rights was over. This undoubtedly eased the way for me.

I had one child in 1953 and another in 1955, but I continued to work, partly because I was able to get inexpensive full-time household help and because we lived near the office. In 1956, my husband decided to leave the UN, and he took a job in Los Angeles as a management consultant. It seemed important that my husband gain self-confidence by being the sole breadwinner for a while, until we needed to save regularly in order to send our boys to college. So when we moved west, I ended my career. Our third child was born in 1961 and the high cost of domestic help and the cost and time involved in commuting (we live in a distant suburb) have prevented any plans to resume my career. Young children cannot be left without a mother or an excellent mother substitute.

I grew up believing that life is not complete unless one has a home and family of one's own. Providing love and security for children is, perhaps, the greatest contribution a woman can make. Furthermore, I realized in graduate school that I probably could not pursue a career when I had young children and I believed writing skills could always be used as time permitted. I was not adequately prepared, however, for the psychological shock of giving up a very satisfying career in order to care for the house and children. My career had exceeded my expectations. The past 7 years (with husband, children, and house, sans career) have been frustrating and have involved adjustments that I have not successfully made. I am presently in therapy with a psychiatrist, partly because of this.

My husband, whose attitude toward my working has always been excellent, does not fully appreciate the problems faced by a mother of young children who would like to make full use of her talents. We are presently going through a very disturbed stage. Through psychiatric help for each of us, we hope to avoid separation and divorce. Although I have anticipated returning to employment as soon as the age of my youngest child permits, I probably will have to go back to work a little sooner, if only to help pay for the doctors. I might take part-time employment, probably in my field, though I may have to change the emphasis within it. I doubt that I will have to retrain (as many women who are now going into teaching are doing). But my old skills may need refreshing.

Since I have felt that I *had* to be involved in the world around me, I have compensated for my temporary loss of career by deeply involving myself in civic activities, spending about 40 hours a week on volunteer and organizational work. These have included neighborhood chairman for a church, board member of the League of Women Voters, secretary of educational and charter revision committees, PTA offices, Cub Scout den mother, and founder and officer of a neighborhood association. My work with the League of Women Voters has taken up the bulk of the time devoted to volunteer activities.

I joined these groups in the (vain?) belief that I was "making democracy work." I like contributing to community betterment and associating with other like-minded people, and my writing skills have been very useful, but the work forces one to endure frustrations while bringing about change—and, oh, the time involved! My life got so out of balance that last spring I decided to take a sabbatical from these activities and reevaluate where I was going. With all the volunteer work, time didn't permit leisure activities, except for a little music, a little bridge. That's one reason my life began to get out of whack, because I chose (foolishly?) to devote my "spare" time to the more important things in life.

Of course, homemaking does have its gratifications, particularly rearing three handsome, intelligent, lovable sons. I like to cook, too. At least that's creative. And I enjoy entertaining. On the other hand, although I like to see floors and shelves shine, I get no special charge out of doing them myself. One is *never* done. A house cleaned one week has to be cleaned all over again the next (or even the next day with three boys around).

I feel very strongly that women should be treated as human beings and encouraged to achieve a level of education commensurate with their interests and abilities. Those who wish should have careers. More and more married women will work, not alone for the money, but for the other satisfactions that employment brings.

I think, however, that our society has not adequately met the need for nursery schools, day care, and even the right attitude toward women working. I think the curriculum in our universities has not adequately prepared women for what lies ahead. I am encouraged by what is being done at Radcliffe and elsewhere.

I am even heartened by this survey which I am answering. I feel as though my university had thrown me a life line, and I want to implore them not to lose hold of their end! Probably more could be done in the way of scholarships for supplementary education for married women whose careers have been interrupted. Maybe job opportunities through the alumni offices could be increased. Of equal importance, certainly, are studies like this one on "life styles of educated women." I personally feel that much of whatever it was that I had to contribute to the world has been submerged in the past several years. Partly because of these frustrations, I presently stand in danger of having my marriage dissolve and the family fall apart. I am too typical of the modern American woman's dilemma.

SUMMARY

The unsettled are very much aware of the shortcomings within their lives and none of them is willing to accept her present situation as irreparable. Some of them have unresolved emotional problems which seem to permeate their entire lives and these may be basic to their discontent. Nevertheless, in no case does it appear that their difficulties are so fundamental as to impede a search for solutions.

While most of these women are in their early forties and an important segment of their lives is in back of them, they have many years ahead. Time may help them to escape from their unsatisfactory circumstances. The woman who is divorced may remarry and have better luck next time, and the woman who has remained single may still meet a suitable partner. Moreover, a woman who is experiencing stress within her marriage may learn how to resolve her difficulties to her own and to her husband's satisfaction.

Time may also allow those whose careers have not given them their anticipated rewards to find satisfactory solutions. If changes can occur in the complex arena of interpersonal relations, surely they can occur—and possibly more readily—in the world of work. Since all these are women with a high order of intelligence and self awareness, their futures may indeed be brighter.

Afterword: The Longer View

These self-portraits tell us a great deal about these women and about the world in which they live. In addition, we obtain a few clues about what the world of tomorrow may offer coming generations of educated women.

One of the most striking facts about these self-portraits is their great variety. Despite the characteristics that these women have in common and that have made it possible to assign each of them to one of four life patterns, there is recurring evidence of strong individual differences among them. Of course, every human being is unique, no life is lived exactly like another. But in view of the fact that these women, by virtue of their educational achievements, are members of a select minority of all women, one might anticipate greater similarity in the ways in which they have ordered their lives. Yet diversity is characteristic not only of this group but also of the larger group from which they were selected. There are wide differences in their goals and values, in their life circumstances, and in their responses to these circumstances.

Yet it is precisely their extended educational experience that is the origin of the diversity in their life patterns. Women come from different backgrounds and are subject to different influences in their youth. But once a group of women decides, for whatever reasons, to pursue education beyond college, they have available to them a greater number of choices of ways to live their lives than is possessed by other females of their generation, greater indeed than those possessed by most males. For women with less educational preparation have a corresponding limitation upon their choice of styles of life, and men generally have little choice but to make work central to their lives.

These women's educational achievements have placed them in optimal positions to realize their desires and their potentialities. They are in preferred positions in society because their opportunities have been many and varied, as have been the choices they made. No matter what her pattern, each of these women's precise method of self realization is highly individual.

Some have followed the path of tradition. They married early and have concentrated on rearing their children. Others have responded quite differently. Some did not marry; others who married decided to remain childless; still others postponed marriage in order to complete their studies.

Just as different are the ways in which these women have handled their career goals. Some have found it easy to renounce their work in favor of homemaking and childrearing, while others have found it important to work outside their homes. Some have worked continuously, others intermittently, and still others have resumed careers after spending periods at home with their children. And each of these groups contains individuals who differ from one another in still other ways.

The men they married hold quite diverse views about the kind of lives they want to lead and want their wives to lead. A few have encouraged their wives to focus upon their careers and to forego having children. At the opposite extreme are men who believe that their children's needs are best served by having their mothers always present. Still other husbands understand their wives' desire to continue in the world of work, and they are willing to assume duties around the home that in earlier generations have been the exclusive province of women. In some families it is the husband who has taken the initiative in encouraging his wife to return to study and to work and who has supported her every inch of the way.

Middle class women with less education tend to be home-makers exclusively because their opportunities in the labor market are limited to low-level jobs. They may consider work, but are disinclined to accept a job when the routine nature of the work open to them brings less satisfaction than do home-centered activities. On the other hand, the more education a woman has, the greater is her attachment to work because the more attractive are her work opportunities. And once exposed to a high degree of intellectual stimulation, many highly edu-cated women fight tenaciously to utilize their knowledge and training.

Thus, the women in this group, alike in their acquisition of education beyond college, also are alike in their strong attach-ment to the world of work. Their education is a valuable asset; many of them are able to engage in fields of endeavor where they can deepen and broaden their knowledge and are often able to make important social contributions. Yet, as they have demonstrated themselves, this work attachment takes many forms. Unlike their sisters, who are usually confined to a small range of job opportunities, and unlike their brothers, who are usually limited to continuous work at full-time jobs, these women exhibit a remarkable number of methods of realizing their occupational interests and objectives.

Although not every woman has been able to make an easy transition from education to work, most of them have suc-ceeded; some immediately, some after reassessment of their goals and adaptation to new circumstances. For the most part, their work tends to strengthen and reenforce their bonds to their fields.

In making successful transitions from the classroom to the world of work, these young women were fortunate be-cause they entered adulthood coincident with the advent of

World War II, which ushered in major changes in social attitudes toward careers for married women. From a position of hostility toward middle-class mothers who sought to work, society began to change to acceptance of the fact that talented women would desire to put their education and skills to use. While some women have found that it is not desirable for them to continue working after they have had children, many are able to keep a foot in both worlds—that of home and of job.

Thus, educational opportunity, the expansion of the job market with its corresponding decrease in discrimination toward women, and the social revolution that brought about a tolerant, almost positive, attitude toward married women working, have been the three major factors that have helped to give shape and definition to the environment in which these educated women must find their ways and make places for themselves.

There is little indeed in these autobiographies to support the widespread impression that education, especially graduate education, is a certain prelude to a woman's unhappiness. It is a widely held belief that her education will either deflect her from marrying and having children, which will inevitably deprive her of the traditional feminine ways of finding gratification or, that if she marries and has a family, she will become frustrated by having to stay at home, bound to tasks of domesticity or, that if she seeks to combine home and job, she will feel guilty if she leaves her children and she will feel dissatisfied with her work since she cannot invest all of her time and energies in her career.

It is difficult indeed to apply this dogma to the facts that emerge from a reading of these self-portraits; in fact, it cannot be applied to them. While there are single women who regret that they have not married and have not had families, there are also many unmarried women who are satisfied with their personal lives and who have found much gratification from their work. Similarly, although a few of the mothers who work feel guilty about leaving their children to the care of others, many go to work and return home with quite different feelings. They believe that they are better wives because of their own work and that they have more patience and understanding for their offspring because they have not been with them for the entire day. While an occasional woman is disappointed because she has been unable to make as rapid progress as she had hoped toward realizing her career objectives because of family commitments, most have been able to work out a satisfactory balance between home and job. This has frequently required that they lower their original occupational sights, but they have been able to accommodate themselves to this. It has often been possible to reset their career sights after their home responsibilities have lightened.

For the most part these educated women are satisfied with their lives. They may not have achieved all they once dreamed about and hoped for, but they have achieved a great deal. They are intelligent enough to appreciate that every satisfaction has its cost. They recognize that a large happy family and a highly successful career are likely to be mutually exclusive. But they also realize that they can be good wives and mothers and, at the same time, have a life outside of their homes in which they can make use of their education and fulfill their interests. There has been a search for balance, and most of them are satisfied with the resolution which they have achieved. Some are still searching.

Since these women represent such a small group in our society, the question of the relevance of their experience for future development of the society at large is a valid one. It is not easy to estimate the shape of the future from events in the past, especially during a period of revolutionary change, when we know that the future will differ substantially from the past. But these autobiographies cast a broad shadow ahead.

There are several institutional changes under way which will undoubtedly help to establish the parameters within which women's future patterns will be shaped. More and more women are or shall be attending graduate schools; more and more openings are becoming available in professional and highly technical occupations. More and more employers are beginning to recognize the existence of a skilled pool of women who are eager to enter the labor market and who show every evidence of a high degree of stability. More and more Americans are recognizing that if women are given increased educational opportunities, they must be granted increased opportunities to utilize that education in all spheres of life. Finally, more and more men and women are coming to realize that work and homemaking can be successfully combined.

On the other hand, our society is affluent enough to permit the educated woman to choose to spend her time at home despite the high social cost of her training. Unlike men, she can make this decision without facing public disapproval. However, the clear and unequivocal drift toward more education for women as for men is a fact. If the pull toward work is a function of greater involvement in education, we must anticipate the involvement of ever more women in the various forms of work attachment that have been delineated here.

Furthermore, if the hours of work for everyone are significantly reduced, as appears probable in the years ahead, this may leave its imprint on the lives of educated women. More and more of them will be able to combine home and work if the hours that they must devote to their jobs are significantly lowered. Yet there are some limits to this development, for the demands of some fields, often those at the highest skill level, do not easily lend themselves to decreased working time. Writing, research, and professional practice, for example, often cannot be scheduled in the same way as other types of work and other means may have to be found to permit women to fulfill these functions satisfactorily.

The current trend toward smaller families will make it easier for a woman to combine family responsibilities and career requirements. She may leave her job for a time, but with a small family she is not faced with the necessity of staying home for such long periods that she finds herself out of touch with developments in her field and out of contact with the world of work. If this trend continues, more and more women will probably seek to enter or reenter the labor market while they are still in their thirties.

The steady gains in preventive and therapeutic health services will lead to continuing reduction in sickness and in the prolongation of life. Women now live an average of 7 years longer than men. More and more of them reach their late years in good mental and physical health. The prospect of many years of productive work draws mature women back to the labor market. Since many of these returnees will have been out of the world of work for long periods, perhaps the future will bring more flexibility in provisions for reentering and withdrawing from work to suit their special needs.

Despite the number of forces that are still operating to increase the participation of educated women in the world of work, there are difficulties that go beyond the nature of work or the dual functions of women that set limits on the activities of even the most highly trained women.

Our society is still not sufficiently geared to permit women to realize fully their potentialities. We are still in a process of transition from the purely maternal role once expected of women to full recognition of women's right to function creatively in the same manner as men. At the same time that we exalt the role of the mother, we deprecate the role of the mother substitute, thereby making mothers reluctant to pursue careers. At the same time that we deplore shortages at the top of the occupational scale, there is still considerable reluctance to hire, assign, and promote capable women to these positions, and to pay them salaries commensurate with those of their male counterparts. At the same time that we take legislative recognition of women's rights to equal employment, we are unwilling to hire them for certain types of administrative positions because business lore insists they are not equal to the demands of these jobs.

Yet, despite the barriers that still prevent women from fully exercising their capacities in all spheres of life, the evidence in these portraits suggests that many of them are heading in that direction. Actually, the life histories of these women demonstrate that society is in a transitional stage with respect to the woman's role.

There are some women who have spent their adult lives thus far primarily engaging in home-centered activities. These may be said to be the traditionalists. Then there are the transitionalists, those women who have either combined homemaking with reduced working schedules or who have already turned to full-time work after a hiatus at home. These women typify society's slow acceptance of new roles. Those women who planned for continuous full-time careers and who have succeeded in this goal may be called the innovators. These innovators' pattern of life resembles most closely that of men. It is a pattern, however, that is not yet fully accepted by society. While the transitionalists and innovators are no longer pioneers, it should be an objective of society to relieve unnecessary strains imposed on them by outmoded attitudes and social policies, and to establish them as valued citizens.

Since the future will see more highly educated women, we may assume that many will be planners who will still plan for either careers or families or both; others will still exercise their prerogative to change their minds; and other women, as most do now, will still be prepared to adapt themselves to changing circumstances. The chances are that they will be highly satisfied women and that they will surmount their hardships because they are aware enough to seek the means to new solutions. Our society will be served best by permitting all of its citizens to fulfill themselves to the extent of their needs and abilities. It seems reasonable to assume that with the passage of time the educated woman will still have a wide variety of ways to design her life and that her career plans will receive greater support and acceptance.